CU00704730

WHAT A STORY!

Mary Underwood

Oxford University Press

Oxford University Press, Walton Street, Oxford OX2 6DP

OXFORD NEW YORK TORONTO
DELHI BOMBAY CALCUTTA MADRAS KARACHI
PETALING JAYA SINGAPORE HONG KONG TOKYO
NAIROBI DAR ES SALAAM CAPE TOWN
MELBOURNE AUCKLAND

and associated companies in
BEIRUT BERLIN IBADAN NICOSIA

Oxford is a trade mark of Oxford University Press

ISBN 0 19 457020 7 Student's Book

ISBN 0 19 457021 5 Teacher's Book

Printed in Hong Kong

Contents

Introduction

What a Story! is a set of twenty units of aural comprehension practice, with additional exercises based on the tapes. Like *Listen to This!* (by the same author and published by Oxford University Press), the units are intended for the intermediate student, who may have studied English at school in his own country for some years, or has spent a year or two studying in England. They give the student preparing for the Cambridge First Certificate in English valuable practice for the examination. The tapes are particularly useful to the student who has little opportunity to hear English speakers.

The Aim
The *aim* of these units is to teach the student to listen effectively and to enable him to select the information he requires from what he hears. The emphasis is on the student's rôle as 'listener'. The use of real (unscripted) speech gives the student the opportunity to experience the ordinary, everyday language of the native speaker, which he is unlikely to find in the usual class situation, where he probably meets a more deliberately patterned type of language.

The Material
There are two tapes containing twenty stories told by native speakers. Each story is between 3½ and 8½ minutes in length and is told by a person or persons involved in, or closely associated with, the events of the story.

The speakers come from various parts of the British Isles, so the student has the opportunity to hear a wide selection of voices and accents.

The order of the stories has been determined by the degree of difficulty the student is likely to experience in listening to them, from the point of view of content, vocabulary, accent, speed and so on.

The first two exercises of each unit are designed to train the student to listen 'extensively' in order to gain the information content of the story, rather than 'intensively', trying to understand every word. He will, therefore, learn to ignore the repetitions, hesitations and interruptions which are characteristic of everyday speech, and develop his comprehension 'span'.

The *Student's Book* contains the relevant work material for each of the taped extracts. It does *NOT* contain the tapescript. The answers to Exercises I and II for each unit are at the end of the book; the answers to the remaining exercises are in the *Teacher's Book*.

For each unit, there is a very brief introductory paragraph, followed by a set of Exercises. Exercise I of each unit is a multiple-choice exercise, where the student simply writes down the correct answer from a selection of possible answers.

Exercise II is a set of 'open' questions, where the student must formulate the answer for himself. Exercises III to VI (or VII) are a variety of related activities, some of which necessitate the use of the tape (and are marked with headphones), whilst others can be done without further reference to the recording.

Using the Tapes and the Book
1 The *brief introductory paragraph* at the beginning of each unit *should be read* before the tape is listened to, as it will focus attention on the type of story which is to follow. In some cases, a note has been added at the end of this paragraph to explain a point which is likely to cause particular difficulty for the student.

2 *The tape should* then *be listened to* carefully, preferably without stopping. This gives the student the opportunity to accustom himself to the voices and to get some idea of the content of the story. [With more advanced students, this step could be omitted.] Some students may find it advantageous to look at the questions in Exercises I and II before listening to the tape or while listening to it, but at this stage it is probably best not to be concerned with the questions at all.

3 Now the student can replay his tape and *find the answers to the multiple-choice questions.* These questions should be done first as it is probably easier for the learner to choose an answer from a selection of four before dealing with the problems of producing his own written answer, as is the case in the second exercise.

4 Having completed the first exercise, the student must now *answer the open questions* in Exercise II. He may make hasty notes and then write his full answers after completing all the questions. He may find it more practicable to stop the tape and write the full answer straight away. How 'complete' his answers are will depend on (*a*) his ability to find the answers, (*b*) what his teacher demands of him, bearing in mind that the aim of the exercise is to train the skill of understanding, not the skill of composing a written answer, and (*c*) whether he is able to control his tape independently of other students (that is—whether he is alone in a language laboratory or at home, or whether he is a member of a class or group with a single tape-recorder.)

5 The function of Exercises I and II is to direct the student's attention to 'focal points' on the tape, so that he will learn to listen effectively for the information he is seeking. They are *not test* items, but aids to comprehension practice.

6 The student should ideally be able to seek *advice* and *guidance* from his teacher at any time while he is carrying out the exercise.

7 In the answers, the actual words spoken on the tape are italicised, so that a *student who makes a mistake* can listen to the tape again and identify the answer which he should have found.

8 The remainder of the exercises in each unit cover *a variety of activities, each related* in some way *to the story* just heard. The teacher will determine how to use these exercises in the light of the level of the class and the time available. Each exercise can be done simply as a practice in itself, or it can be used as the basis of explanation for the skill involved.

The exercises marked with headphones are those which cannot be completed without a tape-recorder. In some situations, it might be easier to do these exercises first, (while still in the language laboratory, for example) and leave the others until later.

9 Advanced students may be able to follow the exercises in the book by giving an *oral summary* of the story as additional practice. It will probably be necessary for a student doing this exercise to make a few notes before beginning so that he does not forget important elements of the story or spoil it by getting the various events in the wrong order.

Acknowledgements for photographs

We are grateful to the following for their help in supplying photographs:
Associated Press (Unit 19); Camera Press (Units 14 and 16);
J. Allan Cash (Unit 3); James Meyer (Units 4, 5, 7, 11 and 17);
Paul Popper (Unit 10); Wing-Commander G.F. Turnbull O.B.E. (Unit 9).

I would like to thank the many people who allowed me to record their stories. My particular thanks are due to my husband who spent a great deal of time helping with recording and with checking the manuscript, and to Mrs Joan Ager who typed the manuscript and gave valuable assistance with the transcription of the taped material.

1 The Lucky Story of the Holiday Money

People on holiday sometimes worry unnecessarily about things going wrong in a foreign country: losing their money, having their passports stolen, and so on. When Mary, John and their family went abroad for a camping holiday, they had good reason to worry ...

 I *Listen to Mary telling Tom her lucky story and answer the following questions by choosing the right answer from* **A B C** *or* **D**.

1 Tom
   A didn't know Mary ever camped
   B thought it was Mary's first camping holiday
   C knew that Mary always camped for her holidays
   D didn't know whether Mary camped or not

2 They stopped in a town
   A to get petrol
   B because there was a camp-site there
   C because they saw a camp-site
   D to look for their folder

3 The camp-site was
   A next to the garage   C a few miles from the garage
   B in the town   D far away

4 The camping 'ticket' enables a person
   A to enter a camp-site   C to belong to a camping club
   B to stay on sites abroad   D to get cheaper rates on a site

5 Mary said that
A no money
B £100
C some hundreds of pounds
D a few pounds
was involved in the loss.

6 The policeman at the police station advised them
A to do nothing about it
B to see the British Consul that day
C to ring the British Consul
D to see the British Consul on the following Monday

7 John distracted the garage man's attention, while Mary
A talked to the policeman
B asked someone else about the camp-site
C looked through the papers on his desk
D found the folder easily

8 Even when they heard their folder had been found, Mary and John were still worried because
A they thought their money might have been stolen out of it
B they thought their passports might have gone
C it might not have been the right folder
D they had to go to the address which the caller left for them

9 The brothers at the cycle-repair shop told Mary and John that they had
A found the folder at the garage
B seen the folder fall off the car
C followed the car to the camp-site
D seen the tent fall off the car

10 John and Mary gave half of their French currency to the brothers as a reward. The other half they
A put in the tent
B gave to the small boy
C gave to the camp-site
D spent on a celebration

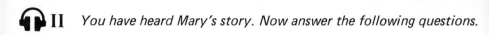

II *You have heard Mary's story. Now answer the following questions.*

1   Where did Mary and her family go on holiday?
2   Why did Mary decide to put all their money and documents together in a folder?
3   What does Mary tell Tom she put in the folder?
4   What was their *real* reason for stopping at the garage?
5   What did the family do to try and find the folder when they were at the camp-site?
6   Why did the family go back to the town?
7   Why did they go back to the garage?
8   How did they persuade the old woman to move from the window-ledge so that they could see what she was sitting on?
9   What was the good news which John and Mary received when they went back to the camp-site?
10 What made the brothers realize the car was going to the local camp-site?

III *You will now hear a single word, which will be said twice. From the list of possible explanations, write down the one which best explains the word.*

1   A collected together in a case   C pushed
    B chosen   D ate like a bird

2   A fixed charges   C small unpleasant animals
    B expresses in written form   D food grown in paddy-fields

3   A ask for   C wager
    B opposite to front   D place for sleeping

4   A learned
    B remained motionless (on the feet)
    C ought to
    D unexpected

5   A encountered
     B would perhaps
     C for wiping the feet on at the door
     D male beings

6   A funny man
     B a grey or white patch in the sky
     C demand (e.g. one's rights)
     D free from dirt

7   A move backwards and forwards
     B suspended
     C long-necked bird
     D moved along in the water

8   A light brownish-yellow colour
     B instrument used for talking at a distance
     C bright
     D experience

9   A destiny
     B lowest part of the leg, below the ankle
     C struggle
     D suit

10   A narrow break
      B wrote down the letters of a word
      C outer edges of the mouth
      D flowed over

IV *Many verbs have nouns which are derived from them. Look at the examples below and then complete the exercise.*
    E.g. (i) to be ....
           Answer: *a being*
       (ii) to camp ....
           Answer: *a camp*

1	to disappoint	9	to agree ....
2	to find	10	to distract ....
3	to pay	11	to move ....
4	to see	12	to feel ....
5	to say	13	to worry ....
6	to do	14	to fall ....
7	to open	15	to guess ....
8	to think	16	to celebrate ....

V *Complete the following, having looked at the example.*
E.g. (i) He comes from France. He is a ....
Answer: *Frenchman*
(ii) He comes from Spain. He is a ....
Answer: *Spaniard*

1 He comes from Italy. He is an ....
2 He comes from Sweden. He is a ....
3 He comes from Norway. He is a ....
4 He comes from Finland. He is a ....
5 He comes from Denmark. He is a ....
6 He comes from Germany. He is a ....
7 He comes from Russia. He is a ....
8 He comes from Scotland. He is a ....
9 He comes from Ireland. He is an ....
10 He comes from Poland. He is a ....
11 He comes from Holland. He is a ....
12 He comes from Belgium. He is a ....
13 He comes from Hungary. He is a ....
14 He comes from Greece. He is a ....
15 He comes from Canada. He is a ....

VI *Look at the pictures and, bearing in mind the story, write down what the people* might *be saying.*

MARY: (having tidied up all the papers in the car)

MARY: (suddenly thinking they must have left the folder at the garage)

JOHN: (to garage man)

MARY: (to old woman)

MAN IN CYCLE-REPAIR SHOP: (explaining how he and his brother found the folder)

Whether one believes in ghosts or not, it is always a bit worrying to hear one's friends telling ghost stories. Although nowadays we hear of ghosts appearing in modern homes, the traditional ghost story is set in a large, rambling, country house, far away from other houses . . .

2 The Mysterious Events at a Country House

▲ I   *Listen to Brian's mysterious story and answer the following
questions by choosing the right answer from* **A B C** *or* **D.**

1   Brian
    A believes in ghosts   **C** doesn't believe in ghosts
    B has seen a ghost   **D** isn't sure about ghosts

2   The big house in Sussex belonged to
    A Brian   **C** Brian's mother's friends
    B Brian's friends   **D** Brian's friend's mother

3   The owners of the house wanted to go to Chichester for the
    week-end
    A to enjoy the coast
    B to sail
    C to sell the house
    D to leave the house unoccupied

4   The weather that summer had been
    A good   **C** mixed
    B bad   **D** exceptional

5   Brian says that when the wind blew through the trees round the
    house they
    A whistled and whimpered   **C** just whistled
    B whistled and whispered   **D** wilted and whispered

6   The old house creaked on a windy night because
    A all the trees made a noise   C it was partly made of wood
    B it was an unfriendly house   D the people had gone away

7   When she opened the door, Brian's mother saw
    A a business man   C a policeman
    B a delivery boy   D nobody

8   The stranger had come to the house because
    A his daughter had invited him
    B he wanted to see his daughter
    C his daughter was away
    D he had never seen his daughter

9   After the stranger had gone, according to Brian's mother,
    A the wind began to blow   C the house began to creak
    B the wind died down   D the television went off

10 When Brian tells Ann how his mother described the changed
    weather conditions after the stranger left the house, we get the
    impression that
    A Ann doesn't really believe it
    B Brian doesn't really believe it
    C both of them believe it
    D neither of them really believe it

 II *You have heard Brian's story. Now answer the following questions.*

1   Does Brian's listener, Ann, believe in ghosts?
2   Is Ann impressed by the idea of hearing the story of Brian's
    mother's experience?
3   How far from the coast was the big house in Sussex?
4   Who did the owners think might go to their house if they left it
    unoccupied?
5   Describe the position of the house, according to Brian.

6   What was Brian's mother doing when she heard the knock at the door on Saturday evening?
7   What made Brian's mother think that the man who came to the door was a business man?
8   What exactly did Brian's mother say to the stranger at the door?
9   Why did the man say he wanted to see his daughter?
10   What did the woman say when Brian's mother told her that her father had called the previous evening?

III *Brian describes the stranger who came to the house as 'a very respectable, elderly man'. Fill in suitable adjectives below. Numbers 1–5 should be made pleasing, attractive descriptions. Numbers 6–10 should be made unattractive.*

1   a rather . . . . , ... house
2   a very . . . . , ... lady
3   an exceedingly . . . . , ... teacher
4   a really . . . . , ... child
5   a perfectly . . . . , ... day
6   a rather . . . . , ... house
7   a very . . . . , ... lady
8   an exceedingly . . . . , ... teacher
9   a perfectly . . . . , ... child
10   a rather . . . . , ... day

IV *Listen to the ten extracts from the story and write down exactly what is said. You will hear each one twice.*

V *Brian uses the phrase 'the wind was howling round the house'. Fill in an appropriate word so that each of the sentences describes a feature of the weather.*
    E.g. The . . . . was shining.
         The *sun* was shining.

1   The . . . . was pattering on the window.
2   The . . . . was glittering on the water.
3   The . . . . was glowing as it set.
4   The . . . . were moving fast across the sky.
5   The . . . . were bouncing off the roof.
6   The . . . . covered the ground with a white carpet.
7   The . . . . was very loud.
8   The . . . . caused serious flooding.
9   The . . . . blew the leaves off the trees.
10 The . . . . flashed right overhead.

VI *You will now hear a single word, which will be said twice. From the list of possible explanations, write down the one which best explains the word.*

1   **A** put in order   **C** alter
    B unusual   **D** look hard

2   **A** price
    B the actors in a play
    C got money for (a cheque, for example)
    D land near the sea

3   **A** travelling by boat
    B disposing of for money
    C only
    D removing the outside covering (of peas, for example)

4   **A** foliage   **C** food made from milk
    B pulls   **D** people who steal

5   **A** low sound uttered by someone in pain
    B solitary
    C part of a skeleton
    D moved by the wind

6   **A** you . . . . on a chair   **C** chair, for example
       B placed   **D** the sense used in seeing

7   **A** rather   **C** peaceful
       B leave   **D** peculiar

8   **A** place where animals are kept
       B shape
       C a type of tree
       D solid

9   **A** 6.00 p.m., for example   **C** attempt
       B men's wear   **D** obtain for money

10   **A** cry out   **C** close
       B fire (a gun, for example)   **D** not long

3 The Happy Story of a Tramp

Mrs Healey, the wife of a school headmaster, told this story of the tramp, Mr Rutley, who used to travel around the Cotswold hills in the 1950s and 1960s. You will hear the word 'shilling' in this story. This was the equivalent of 5p before decimalization was introduced in England in 1971. You will also hear Mrs Healey mention the school's production of *The Mikado*. This is a well-known operetta by Gilbert and Sullivan.

I   *Listen to the story and answer the following questions by choosing the right answer from* A B C *or* D.

1   Mr Rutley, the tramp, left his home
   A   when his father left
   B   when his father died
   C   when his mother died
   D   when his father became inadequate

2   Mrs Healey gave Mr Rutley old wellingtons to wear, not shoes, because
   A   she had no shoes to give him
   B   he didn't like shoes
   C   his feet wouldn't fit into shoes
   D   he asked for wellingtons

3   Mr Rutley couldn't receive an old-age pension from the Ministry of Social Security because
   A   he had no fixed address   C   he didn't ask for one himself
   B   he didn't work   D   he lived out of the district

4   The girls at the school got to know Mr Rutley because
     A he lived near the 6th Form College
     B he went to the Domestic Science section
     C they met him along the road with the headmistress
     D Mrs Healey talked about him

5   After Mr Kenlock had got the old caravan, it was painted over the
     weekend by
     A Mr Rutley   C Mr Kenlock
     B the girls   D everybody

6   Mr Kenlock had to tow the caravan with a tractor because
     A it was very heavy   C he had to go down a cart-track
     B he'd just painted it   D it was a bitterly cold day

7   Just before he got his caravan, Mr Rutley had been sleeping
     A in the school   C in a barn
     B on the roadside   D in the woods

8   Mrs Healey thought Mr Rutley shouldn't sleep in the caravan on
     the first night because
     A he should wait a while C he was thrilled
     B he had no cooker   D it smelt of paint

9   Now that Mr Rutley lives in the caravan, he travels to the village
     A by bicycle   C by tricycle
     B on foot   D by car

10   Mrs Healey thinks that Mr Rutley is a nice man because
     A he always pays for what he has
     B he never asks for anything he doesn't need
     C he never needs anything
     D he always takes things he doesn't need

II *You have listened to the story about Mr Rutley; now answer the following questions, please.*

1 Why did Mr Rutley's circle of travel become smaller?
2 What did Mrs Healey from the school give Mr Rutley when she first started to see him in the district?
3 Why did Mrs Healey's husband think that Mr Rutley should be receiving an old-age pension?
4 What did the girls give Mr Rutley when they met him on their way back from Domestic Science lessons?
5 What did the girls do to raise money to buy Mr Rutley a caravan?
6 What does Mr Rutley call the old-fashioned caravan that the school provided for him?
7 How did Mr Kenlock get the caravan from Witney to where the tramp needed it?
8 When the school gave Mr Rutley the caravan it was 'complete with everything'. What does Mrs Healey mention as 'everything'?
9 What was the only thing they hadn't got for Mr Rutley at that time?
10 What does Mr Rutley collect from the village and the school when he goes out every Monday?

III *Give an explanation of each of the following words or phrases as it is used on the tape.*

1 illiterate
2 took to the roads
3 tremendous
4 intermittently
5 deformed
6 dying to
7 of no fixed abode
8 contribute
9 cosy
10 to site it

IV *The phrase 'as straight as a soldier' is not a very common one. Others of this type are better known. Complete the following examples.*

1 as white as . . . .
2 as green as . . . .
3 as thin as . . . .
4 as happy as . . . .
5 as sober as . . . .

V *Now listen to the tape, Exercise V. Write down the three words or groups of words in the order in which they are spoken. Listen very carefully! You will hear each set of words twice. There are five questions.*

VI *You will now hear a single word, which will be said twice. From the list of possible explanations, write down the one which best explains the word.*

1 **A** collection of stamps (for example) of the same sort
   B spoke the words
   C unhappy
   D small hut

2 **A** the whole
   B to do with kings and queens
   C thick liquid which floats on water
   D long shaped stick used to row a boat

3 **A** the same as   **C** after the right time
   B a large area of water   **D** not heavy

4 **A** a small area of still water   **C** drag
   B the male equivalent of a cow **D** cause to bubble with heat

24

5   A certain manner of doing anything
     B old, when referring to bread
     C take without permission
     D even now

VII *You will now hear a sentence spoken in a particular way. It will be spoken twice. Look at the groups of possible answers and choose the one which best explains why the sentence is spoken like that.*

1   A I don't believe you at all.
     B I didn't believe you last time.
     C I usually believe other people rather than you.
     D I believe you, even if nobody else does.

2   A I haven't ever believed you before.
     B I usually believe other people rather than you.
     C I don't believe you at all.
     D I always believe everyone.

3   A I doubted you before.
     B I believe you even if nobody else does.
     C I always believe everyone.
     D I don't believe you.

4   A I usually believe other people rather than you.
     B You haven't ever believed me.
     C You know I always believe you.
     D I didn't believe you last time.

Now you will hear the four sentences again so that you can check your answers.

4 The Frightening Consequences of Finding a Body

The experience which Liz had was a most unpleasant affair and it's no wonder that she was frightened. It happened while she was living abroad and that made it even worse, because it is always hard to understand the operation of the law in a foreign country.

Liz mentions the C.I.D. which is the Criminal Investigation Department of the police force in England. Of course, the equivalent in another country would not be called the C.I.D., but for an English person it is quite usual to say C.I.D., meaning the special department which deals with crime.

I   *Listen to Liz's frightening story and answer the following questions by choosing the right answer from* **A B C** *or* **D**.

1   Liz says she was quite frightened when she saw the body in the road because
   A she thought it was a dead body
   B it was spread-eagled in the road
   C bodies are sometimes used in ambushes there
   D she thought she had hit the man

2   Liz describes the man's condition. Which of the following is untrue?
   A He was alive.   **C** He had been attacked.
   B He was conscious.   **D** He was drunk.

3   When they got to the hospital with the man
    A a doctor came out to meet them
    B they were helped immediately
    C nobody at all was there
    D they were told to go to another hospital

4   Liz got terribly angry with the nurse at the hospital because
    A the nurse opened the car door
    B she is bad-tempered
    C she couldn't find a registration form
    D the nurse walked off and didn't help the man

5   The doctor recommended Liz
    A to be very nice   C to call the police
    B to go   D to phone the hospital next day

6   The police got to know that Liz was the one who had taken the
    man to the hospital because
    A they had taken her phone number
    B the doctor who treated the man told them
    C they were traffic policemen who checked car numbers
    D the nurse had given them Liz's car number

7   When Liz was taken to the police station
    A she was locked in a cell
    B she was questioned and then locked up
    C she was questioned and then released
    D she was told that Michael was guilty

8   The Consul had to ask the Vice-Consul to help because
    A the Consul was new and hadn't had a case like this before and
       the Vice-Consul was used to the country
    B he did not know what sort of a charge had been made against
       Liz

C he thought the Ambassador would want to know
D the Ambassador made representations

9   Liz was the obvious person to accuse of the murder, after the real murderer had bribed the police, because she had
   A been in the bar   **C** been to a dance
   B seen the fight   **D** taken the man to the hospital

10 Liz left the country soon after the incident because
   A the Ambassador advised her to
   B she had packed up
   C her money was blocked
   D she couldn't get an exit visa

II   *Now that you have heard the story, please answer the following questions.*

1   At what time did the incident begin?
2   What made Liz decide that they were not about to be ambushed when they saw the body in the road?
3   Was Liz alone when she came across the body in the road?
4   Why was it difficult to get the man into the car?
5   Why was it never possible to ask the man what had happened to him?
6   Liz had to make a complete statement to the police. What examples does she give of the sort of detail they wanted?
7   What did the police say Liz had done to the man when she was taken to the police station?
8   What sort of charge was made against Liz?
9   How did Liz go to the police station the following day?
10 Who had told the police who the real murderer was?

III *In the story the man had been stabbed with a knife. Complete the following by adding a verb in the correct tense. (They are not all nasty!)*

E.g. If I had had a feather, I could . . . . him.
    Answer: *have tickled.*

1   If I had a gun, I could . . . . the man.
2   If I had had a stick, I could . . . . her.
3   If I had had more food, I could . . . . them all.
4   If I had had a pen, I could . . . . to mother.
5   If I had a camera, I could . . . . the lady.
6   If I had a spare room, I could . . . . him.
7   If I had had a car, I could . . . . them all.
8   If I had enough money, I could . . . . them all.
9   If I had enough speed, I could . . . . him.
10 If I had had her number, I could . . . . her.

 IV *List at least 15 people (or groups of people) who are mentioned on the tape and describe each one in a few words, starting the description with 'who'. E.g. 'Liz, who found the body'.*

 V *Use each of the following words and phrases from the story in a sentence of your own to show that you understand what it means.*

1   spread-eagled
2   ambush
3   a decoy
4   unconscious
5   brutally assaulted
6   slumped
7   lost my temper

8 found out
9 kind-hearted
10 arrested
11 interrogated
12 wounds
13 panicked
14 took charge
15 lawyer
16 victim
17 bribed
18 to pick upon
19 packed up
20 blocked

VI *List five facts that you have learned about Liz from listening to this tape.*

5 An Embarrassing Moment for John

Many people don't like lifts because they are afraid that the lift will stop between two floors and they will be trapped inside. John's story is about a lift, but he didn't get stuck inside it. You could say that he got stuck *outside* the lift! He tells how his situation became more and more embarrassing as time went on.

I *Listen to the story and answer the following questions by choosing the right answer from A B C or D.*

1   John's knowledge of Swedish was
    A bad   C excellent
    B good   D non-existent

2   John should have pressed the button for the fourth floor when he got into the lift at his block of flats because
    A his wife-to-be lived there
    B he was tired
    C he lived on the fourth floor
    D he wanted to visit someone on the fourth floor

3   John was surprised when the lift passed the fourth floor because
    A it didn't stop
    B the lady who lived next door to him was waiting there
    C he lived on the fifth floor
    D there was a man and woman waiting there

4   John thought the lady who lived next door to him
     A lived alone   C had lots of visitors
     B lived with her family   D was married

5   John didn't walk back down to the fourth floor because
     A he wanted to visit someone on the fifth floor
     B the man and woman had gone to the ground floor
     C he would look foolish
     D there were no stairs to walk down

6   When he got out of the lift, John decided to wait on the fifth
     floor until
     A the man and woman came up
     B the man had gone
     C someone came out of the lift
     D the lift came back up again

7   John made a noise, which echoed down the stairs, when
     A he opened a door
     B he began to walk across the floor
     C the carpet slipped
     D he went into the attic

8   He looked out of the window at
     A the lights of Stockholm   C the man and the woman
     B another block of flats   D the dark night

9   The man who came to investigate didn't understand John because
     A John spoke to the woman   C the man was Swedish
     B John spoke nonsense to him D John spoke in English

10   When John took out his keys the man stepped back because
     A somebody called him
     B the lift arrived
     C one of the doors of the flats opened
     D he thought John had a gun

II   *You have heard John's story; now answer the following questions, please.*

1   Where exactly did John's future wife live when they were both in Sweden?
2   What time did John come home on the evening he describes?
3   How did John know that the man waiting for the lift was about to leave?
4   On what floor did John get out of the lift?
5   Why didn't John send the lift back to the ground floor?
6   Why did John wait and wait and wait on the fifth floor?
7   Why did John have to hop across the landing?
8   What does John say he felt like when the man started to come up the stairs from the floor below?
9   Why did John want the man to follow him?
10   What exactly did John say to the man before he closed the door of his own flat?

III   *Give an explanation of each of the following phrases as it is used on the tape.*

1   The lift sailed up
2   a man was about to leave
3   I must have been distracted
4   In a sort of reflex way, I got out of the lift
5   my fatal error
6   let myself in
7   I heard whispering
8   to work out what was going on
9   to make a clean breast of it
10   I must have talked gibberish
11   I reached for my pocket
12   beckoned to him

IV *John came home between 11.00 p.m. and midnight. Write in full the times shown below.*

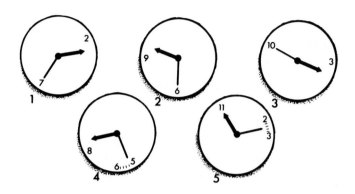

V *You will now hear a single word, which will be said twice. Choose the answer which best explains the word.*

1   **A** make musical sounds with the voice
     B used for flying
     C (an) object
     D fetch

2   **A** not early, nor on time   **C** the one that comes at the end
     B easy to carry   **D** allow

3   **A** a building consisting of a number of flats
     B dark colour
     C say something is someone's fault
     D opposite to front

4   **A** edge of the sea   **C** footwear
     B not fast   **D** exhibition for people to see

5   **A** took hold of   **C** wound round (like hair)
     B named   **D** made less hot

VI *John was in Sweden and spoke Swedish. Please complete the following in the same way.*

1   Peter was in Spain and spoke . . . .
2   John was in Russia and spoke . . . .
3   Michael was in France and spoke . . . .
4   Paul was in Germany and spoke . . . .
5   Susan was in Greece and spoke . . . .
6   James was in Hungary and spoke . . . .
7   Mary was in China and spoke . . . .
8   Sarah was in Holland and spoke . . . .
9   Brian was in Japan and spoke . . . .
10 Charles was in Denmark and spoke . . . .

VII *John went to the fifth floor instead of the fourth floor. Here are some buttons in a lift, (in a very high building). Write in full the floors which they show.*
E.g. (10)—the tenth floor

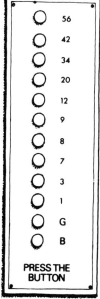

VIII *John took his keys out of his pocket. Write down everything you have in your pocket (or in your handbag or purse).*

6 The Sad Life of an Old Man

Linda's job is concerned with social service. She meets all kinds of people in her work—mainly people who have difficulties of one sort or another and need help. The story is about one of these unfortunate people, although his suffering is not caused by any of the problems she usually meets.

 I *Listen to the sad story and answer the following questions by choosing the right answer from **A B C** or **D**.*

1 Linda went to see the old man
   A because he lived in bad conditions
   B because he was old
   C because he asked her to
   D because he was poor

2 The old man's house
   A was modern   **C** was not like Linda expected
   B was fashionable   **D** was large, as Linda expected

3 Mr Sinclair, the old man
   A didn't live in his house
   B lived in part of his house
   C let part of his house
   D used his whole house for himself

4 Mr Sinclair
   A was fit   **C** was very likeable
   B was weak   **D** had a bad shoulder

5   Linda went to visit Mr Sinclair again because
     A she wanted to write her report about him
     B she kept thinking about him
     C it was usual to go back a second time
     D he telephoned and asked her to go again

6   After his parents' death, Mr Sinclair took over the family business
     which then
     A collapsed   C floundered
     B went well   D was bought by foreigners

7   After the departure of his sisters, Mr Sinclair
     A got married   C stayed alone
     B moved out of his house D made many friends

8   Mr Sinclair was eventually forced to give up his business because
     A he was well off
     B he began to suffer from arthritis
     C his arthritis got worse and worse
     D he was completely alone

9   While telling Linda about his past life, Mr Sinclair was
     A unhappy   C thrilled
     B excited   D respected

10   Mr Sinclair really wanted
     A more money   C to have more friends
     B to have visitors   D to be young again

II   *Now that you have heard Linda's sad story, please answer the
     following questions.*

1   What was the survey about?
2   How does Linda describe some of the people she had already
     seen in connection with the survey?

3 What sort of thing did Mr Sinclair grumble about when he talked to Linda?
4 What did Linda do when she left Mr Sinclair's house after her first visit?
5 Was Mr Sinclair from a rich family?
6 When did Mr Sinclair begin to support his two sisters?
7 What did Mr Sinclair's two sisters do which meant that he didn't have to continue to support them?
8 When did Mr Sinclair develop arthritis?
9 How did other people in the area look on Mr Sinclair when he was running his business?
10 What was Mr Sinclair's condition at the time when Linda visited him?

 III *The words and phrases below are taken from Linda's story. For each one, give another word or phrase which means the same. (Words in brackets are sometimes added to help you recognize the phrase.)*

1 We were conducting (a survey)
2 In connection with (this survey)
3 tended to be elderly
4 an air of faded gentility
5 (the rest of the house was) shut up
6 he never stopped grumbling
7 about how the area had gone down
8 and so on and so forth
9 he'd got a real chip on his shoulder
10 he was rather frail
11 not spectacularly rich
12 (his father) had supported his mother
13 it fell to him (to support his sisters)
14 the business began to flourish
15 he acquired new premises
16 (his sister) emigrated

17 he cut himself off (from his friends)
18 he still battled on
19 he was forced to give up
20 to be somebody of note

IV *Listen carefully to the end of the story again. Write down exactly what Linda says about Mr Sinclair.*

V *Below you will see some verbs which were used in the story. Use each one (in the given tense) in a sentence of your own to show that you understand it.*

1	went along	7	left out
2	to let (somebody in)	8	went on
3	to show (somebody) in	9	took (somebody) on
4	went back	10	took over
5	wrote up	11	built up
6	didn't think about	12	cut (himself) off

VI *Mr Sinclair never married. However, imagine he did and complete his family tree, inventing names and a family for him.*

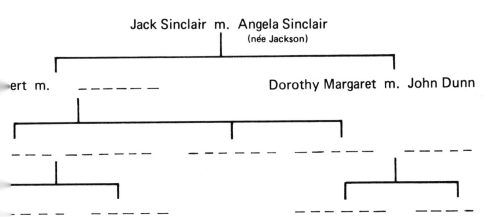

Jack Sinclair m. Angela Sinclair
(née Jackson)

ert m. ――――― Dorothy Margaret m. John Dunn

Now draw your family tree, if possible including at least three generations of your family.

Almost everyone, at one time or another, finds himself in a situation which he would rather have avoided. Brian's experience in Brighton was such an uncomfortable one that he is likely to remember it for many years.

7 An Uncomfortable Situation for Brian

I *Listen to Brian's story and answer the following questions by choosing the right answer from* **A B C** *or* **D**.

1   The Study Centre is
    A a language school   **C** a student hostel
    B a hotel   **D** a conference centre

2   The Director of the School couldn't spend the afternoon with Brian.
    A He was too busy to do so.
    B He was giving the next lecture.
    C He had to stay at the school.
    D He didn't say why he couldn't.

3   The Director expected television programmes for the afternoon to include
    A reading   **C** lectures
    B tennis   **D** football

4   The Director
    A gave Brian his bunch of keys
    B gave Brian two keys
    C selected one key from a bunch for Brian
    D didn't give Brian a key

5   Before he went to the flat, Brian
    A prepared his second lecture   **C** lost the key
    B got another key   **D** had lunch

6   Brian was surprised to find no books
      A in English   **C** on professions
      B on English   **D** at all

7   In one corner of the room, Brian saw
      A books on shelves   **C** chairs on tables
      B models sitting down   **D** experiments set up

8   The man who came to the door asked Brian
      A 'Where's Mr Brooks?'   **C** 'What are you doing here?'
      B 'Is the owner here?'   **D** 'Does Mr Brooks live here?'

9   Which of the following did Brian *not* include in his attempts to
      reply to the man's first question?
      A 'I don't live here.'
      B 'I don't know why I'm here.'
      C 'I'm spending the afternoon here.'
      D 'I'm a friend of Mr Brooks.'

10   Mr Brooks had the key of the flat below his because he was
      A in the habit of using that flat
      B doing their cleaning
      C stupid
      D looking after their dog

11   The furniture was piled up on the table
      A so that Mr Brooks could clean up the dog hairs
      B because Brian was going there
      C to protect it from dog hairs
      D so that Brian could relax

II   *Now that you have heard Brian's story, please answer the follow-
         ing questions.*

1   What were the subjects on which Brian was to lecture at the
      Study Centre?

2 What three things did the Director of the School expect Brian to do at his flat during the afternoon?
3 Where did the Director live?
4 What made Brian feel particularly uncomfortable when he went into the flat?
5 What did Brian think was the meaning of the state of the flat when he went in?
6 What were the subjects of the books which Brian saw on the bookshelves in the flat?
7 Where did Brian sit and read the newspaper?
8 Did Brian have the key to the flat on the top floor?
9 Why was Brian disinclined to spend the rest of the afternoon walking round Brighton?
10 Why was the dog not in the flat when Brian went there?

III *Here are some sentences and phrases from the tape. Use the words in italics in a sentence of your own.*

1 It's called the Study Centre *or something*.
2 It all *went off quite well*.
3 He doesn't really *know which is which*.
4 He *went through* the key ring.
5 I went up to *what I thought was* the top flat.
6 You feel uncomfortable *to start with*.
7 *It looks as if* he's *either* spring-cleaning *or* preparing to go away on holiday.
8 *Not only* were there weird books ...
9 I don't know *what's going on*.
10 The people ... are very *fussy about* their furniture.

IV *Complete the following sentences using a word beginning with with 'un-'.*
E.g. Brian found himself in an *uncomfortable* situation.

1 What an .... room! Everything's everywhere!

45

2   Speak more slowly please. I'm . . . . to understand you.
3   I don't want to read this book any more. It's so . . . .
4   I didn't ask him to come. He just arrived . . . .
5   He didn't even say 'Thank you', the . . . . boy!
6   Try and smooth it out a bit more. It's still far too . . . .
7   He didn't do it on purpose. It was quite . . . .
8   He didn't have to do it. It was quite . . . .
9   I've never seen anything like that. How . . . . it is!
10 Your belt's . . . . Fasten it up!

V   *Complete the sentences by putting the verb in the correct form.*
       E.g. Brian . . . . for ages when Mr Brooks arrived. (to wait)
       Brian *had been waiting* for ages when Mr Brooks arrived.

1   One day last week Brian . . . . to Brighton. (to go)
2   I wonder if you . . . . to go to my flat. (to like)
3   You know how complicated bunches of keys . . . . (to be)
4   Don't worry! I . . . . your flat. (to find)
5   I went to the top flat and . . . . the key. (to take out)
6   I felt uncomfortable because all the furniture . . . . (to pile up)
7   I sat down and . . . . to read the newspaper. (to begin)
8   I . . . . there about ten minutes when I heard a knock at the
    door. (to be)
9   I don't live here. I . . . . the afternoon here. (to spend)
10 I . . . . the dog with me today. (to have)

VI   *You will now hear a sentence spoken in a particular way. It will
        be spoken twice. Choose the phrase which best explains why the
        sentence is spoken like that.*

1   **A** No part of it was weak.   **C** It was not a disaster.
    B It was better at the end.   **D** Some parts of it were weak.

2   **A** No part of it was weak.   **C** Some parts of it were weak.
    B It was all moderately good.   **D** It was not a disaster.

3   A I'm sure I've got the right one somewhere.
    B I think this is the one.
    C This is definitely the one, not that.
    D Maybe this is it.

4   A Maybe this is it.
    B I think this is the right one.
    C I've got the right one.
    D I haven't made a mistake, although I thought for a moment
      I had.
    *Now you will hear the four sentences again, so that you can check
    your answers.*

VII *Write down what is being said in each picture.*

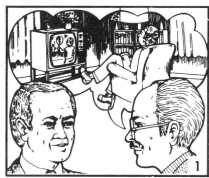

THE DIRECTOR: ....

THE DIRECTOR: ....

THE LANDLORD: ....
AND BRIAN ....

Brian asked Mr Brooks why the
furniture was piled up.
        THE DIRECTOR: ....

47

8 An Alarming Experience on the Road

Road accidents are nearly always caused by a driver's mistake or mis-judgement. Sometimes they occur because of unusual road or weather conditions.

This story is about an accident which had a most unusual and alarming cause.

As a result of the accident, John, who tells the story, was given a 'breathalyser' test by the police. A motorist can be asked to take a test if the police suspect that he has drunk too much alcohol to be able to drive safely. The motorist is asked to blow into a plastic bag through a tube containing coloured crystals. The amount of alcohol in the motorist's breath is shown by the change in the colour of the crystals. If the test is positive, further tests are carried out.

 I   *Listen to John's alarming story and answer the following questions by choosing the right answer from* **A B C** *or* **D**.

1   The Lotus car suddenly slowed down
    A on a dual-carriageway   **C** behind John's car
    B three miles from Norwich   **D** on a two-way road

2   When John realized something was wrong, he
    A stopped behind the Lotus
    B he drove on the kerb
    C he stopped in front of the Lotus
    D he drove on

3   The Lotus suddenly shot forward when
    A John reached the car
    B there was a sound of acceleration
    C John was about five yards from the car
    D John had to leap out of the way

4   John was frightened as the cars, locked together, went down the
    road because
    A another car came round the bend
    B there was a bend and he thought something might come round
       it in the opposite direction
    C there was a head-on collision
    D both cars went across the road

5   John's car finally stopped
    A up a grass bank   C in a shop
    B in a large hedge   D in a ploughed field

6   There was steam everywhere because
    A the Lotus engine was running
    B the radiator of the Lotus had burst
    C it was cloudy
    D people were smoking

7   Having got the driver out of the Lotus, John ran out into the road
    A to get help
    B because he heard a shout for help
    C because help was on its way
    D because people had stopped

8   John and his friend went to the police station because
    A the man was unconscious
    B the police told them to go there
    C the fire brigade arrived
    D John wanted to make a statement

9   The police apologized for giving John a breathalyser test because
     A he wasn't drunk
     B they had wrongly thought that he had been driving the car at
       the time of the crash
     C he made a statement about the accident
     D he told them a story

10   The man in the car had died
     A in the field after the crash
     B in the police car
     C before his car crashed into John's
     D when the car crashed into John's

 II   *You have heard the alarming story, so now please answer the*
         following questions.

1   Why were John and his friend driving to Norwich?
2   What did John notice about the driver of the Lotus when he
     glanced at him as he overtook him?
3   When John had stopped and got out of his car, he and his friend
     walked back towards the Lotus. Which one of them walked on
     the grass verge and which one walked in the road?
4   When the Lotus suddenly shot forward, who or what did it hit
     first?
5   Where did the Lotus finally stop?
6   How was grass and mud being thrown all over the road after the
     cars had stopped moving?
7   When they managed to open the driver's door of the Lotus, they
     got the driver out. What else did they do at the car?
8   Where did John get blankets from?
9   Why was John given a breathalyser test when he got to the police
     station?
10   What news was phoned in to the police station while the state-
     ments were being made?

III *Here are some motoring and road terms. Express them in different words.*

1	dual-carriageway	6	the grass verge
2	two-way road	7	the car was smashed
3	slowed down	8	a head-on collision
4	lay-by	9	turned the ignition off
5	overtake	10	a crash

IV *Listen to the extract from the story and write down exactly what John says.*

V *Below are some groups of short sentences. Join all the sentences in a group together so that they form one sentence. (Do not use 'and' more than once in any group except in number 3.)*

1 John was driving towards Norwich. His friend was with him. They both teach in Norwich.
2 We followed a Lotus car for three or four miles along a dual-carriageway. We entered a two-way road. The Lotus slowed down. There was no apparent reason for this. We overtook the Lotus.
3 I had pulled into the kerb. My passenger got out of the car. I got out of my car. We walked back towards the Lotus. We hadn't reached the car. The car shot forward. It nearly knocked me down.
4 The cars went up the bank together. John's car left the Lotus. John's car went through the hedge. John's car went into a ploughed field. The Lotus was left in the thick part of the hedge.
5 We wanted to get the driver out. We tried to open the passenger door. It was locked. We climbed through the hedge. We got round to the driver's door.

VI *You will now hear words in groups of three. Write down the words in each group in the order in which they are spoken. You will hear each set twice. There are ten questions.*

9 A Remarkable Event Caused by the Wind

To see somebody else in danger and not to be able to do anything about it is a most unpleasant experience. When, as in this case, it is your own daughter who is in danger, the feeling of helplessness is even more acute. On the day when Gerry and his daughter went to make a film for a children's television programme called *Magpie*, just such a situation arose.

I *Listen to Gerry telling a remarkable story about his daughter, Christine, and answer the following questions by choosing the right answer from A B C or D.*

1 Gerry's daughter, Christine, has flown across the Channel twice in
  A we don't know what   **C** a light aircraft
  B a balloon   **D** a harness

2 When using a Humpty Dumpty balloon, the pilot
  A sits in the basket
  B jumps into the basket
  C wears a harness attached to the balloon
  D hangs on to the balloon with his hands

3 When Gerry and his daughter went to Teddington, they weren't keen to begin ballooning immediately, because
  A they were at a studio
  B there were footballers in the park
  C they weren't ready
  D it was windy

4   They attached a rope to
    A Christine's hand   **C** Christine's harness
    B the load-ring of the balloon   **D** the quick-release devices

5   When Gerry shouted 'Cut', Christine
    A didn't hear   **C** cut the rope
    B undid her quick-releases   **D** went up in the air

6   When the rope was snatched out of the hands of those holding it
    by the wind, it
    A wrapped round the balloon
    B simply hit Christine as she lay on the ground
    C wrapped round Christine and picked her up
    D caught in the trees

7   When Gerry saw Christine being carried away, he
    A shouted and tried to follow her
    B ran away
    C called for help from the studio
    D went into the studio

8   The rope unwrapped itself from round Christine
    A when she hit the wire surrounds of the tennis court
    B when Gerry shouted
    C when she hit the side of the studio
    D when she fell

9   Gerry was angry with the ambulance men because
    A he is ill-tempered
    B he was very agitated
    C they didn't come for an hour
    D they took his daughter to hospital

10 Now Christine
    A is still in hospital
    B is perfectly recovered from her accident

C has internal injuries
D has a bad hip

II *Now that you've heard the story, please answer the following questions.*

1 What is exceptional about Gerry's daughter as far as ballooning is concerned?
2 How does one move along when using a Humpty Dumpty balloon?
3 What did 'Brainy' Dodds do in 1920?
4 Why did Gerry and his daughter go to Teddington?
5 Why did the cameramen want Christine to do a little lift-off in spite of the poor weather conditions?
6 What happened at the moment when Christine was just coming down to the ground?
7 How far was Christine below the balloon when it carried her off across the tennis courts?
8 Where did she eventually fall?
9 What condition did Gerry find Christine in when he reached her?
10 What saved Christine from breaking her skull?

III *Find the following words and phrases on the tape and give an explanation for each one as it is used in the story.*

1 float
2 repeat the procedure
3 revived
4 tremendous gust of wind
5 unharmed
6 wrapped round
7 swept her
8 uncoiled
9 shattered
10 borne aloft

IV *Here is the part of the story where Gerry describes what a Humpty Dumpty balloon is. Listen to it and with the help of the phrases below, write down the exact words that he says.*

'She was using a Humpty Dumpty...
That is, ...
You have a harness strapped on you, ..., which is
.... to the bottom of the balloon. And the idea is
.... and you .... and then ....
.... and you ....
It's ....'

V *Gerry explains that 'you fly a balloon'. Complete the following with the appropriate verb.*

1 You .... a cake in the oven.
2 You .... the furniture with furniture-cream.
3 You .... a balloon with hydrogen gas.
4 You .... a cigarette with a match.
5 You .... a tree with a saw.
6 You .... a television with a knob.
7 You .... your way with a map.
8 You .... letters with a pen.
9 You .... eggs in oil.
10 You .... the garden with a spade.
11 You .... the grass with a lawn-mower.
12 You .... the petrol tank with petrol.
13 You .... your books in a bag.
14 You .... the door with a key.
15 You .... flowers in your garden.

VI *Imagine that you are Christine. Write a paragraph (100—130 words) as if in a letter from hospital after the accident, explaining what happened to you from the moment you landed safely on the ground after the first small jump until the time you were taken to hospital.*

10 A Moral Learnt in France

Roulette is a gambling game played in casinos all over the world. It is played with a roulette wheel which has a sort of clock-face with numbered slots all round it. A small ball is thrown into the wheel as it spins. The game is concerned with betting on which numbered slot the ball will come to rest in when the wheel stops spinning. The numbers are all either red or black in colour, and players can also bet on whether the ball will stop at a red coloured number or a black coloured one.

Although Tom wasn't interested in gambling himself, he agreed to go to France with a friend of his, Tim, to try out an 'unbeatable' system for winning at roulette.

N.B. You will notice near the end of the story that Tom accidentally says 'drowned' when he meant to say 'drown'.

I   *Listen to Tom's story and answer the following questions by choosing the right answer from A B C or D.*

1   The story is about a time when
A   Tom was at Oxford University
B   Tom's friend lived with him
C   Tom was at the same university as his friend
D   Tom was at university, but not at Oxford

2   Tom's friend, Tim, sent for all the printed records of the spins of all of the leading casinos on the Continent
A   to persuade himself that his system was right
B   to work out a system
C   to convince Tom that his system was right
D   to discover what the record was

3   Tom went with Tim to Le Touquet because
     A he was sceptical   C Tim wanted a companion
     B he had £75   D he needed the money

4   They went to France for the first day of the casino being open
     because
     A the Marquis of Bath was going
     B the friend was anxious to get there
     C it was out of season
     D the plane wasn't busy

5   When Tom and Tim went to the casino, they wore
     A old casual clothes
     B walking clothes
     C suits
     D clothes which they had borrowed from the hotel

6   When the Marquis of Bath and his wife saw Tom and Tim at the
     casino, they
     A spoke to them
     B invited them to join their group
     C started gambling
     D ignored them

7   By ten to twelve, Tom and Tim had won
     A £200   C nothing
     B £350   D £75

8   To double ten times and not to win was
     A theoretically correct   C convincing
     B impossible   D possible

9   Tom and Tim kept £3 at the end of the evening to
     A buy drinks with   C burn in the wood
     B pay the fare home   D gamble with later

10 In the notebooks which they burnt in the wood, Tim had
A kept his lecture notes
B marked his results for the evening
C worked out the system he thought was unbeatable
D written results for months and months

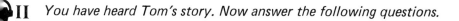

II *You have heard Tom's story. Now answer the following questions.*

1 What did Tom's friend, Tim, think was an unbeatable system for winning at roulette?
2 What was Tom going to get if Tim won money at the casino in Le Touquet?
3 How did Tom and Tim get to somewhere near Le Touquet from England?
4 How many passengers travelled on the plane?
5 How did Tom and Tim manage to be away from the airport and on the road hitching a lift by the time the other passengers came along in their cars?
6 The casino was nearly empty. Who was there, however, when the two students went in?
7 What did Tom and Tim arrange about how long they would continue playing roulette?
8 How did Tom and Tim lose all their money after ten to twelve?
9 What did the two friends do with the notebooks in which Tim had worked out the 'unbeatable' system after they had lost all their money?
10 Why was it a good thing that they lost the money, in Tom's opinion?

III *Tim was not an expert in mathematics (a mathematician) according to Tom. Complete the following according to the subjects.*

1 Beryl is an expert in psychology. She could be called a ....

2   Bob is an expert in philosophy. He could be called a . . . .
3   John's subject is physics. He could be called a . . . .
4   Peter is a specialist in biology. He could be called a . . . .
5   Brian specializes in geography. He could be called a . . . .
6   Nicholas is an expert in history. He could be called a . . . .
7   Richard is a specialist in languages. He could be called a . . . .
8   Philip is an expert in chemistry. He could be called a . . . .

 IV   *Give an explanation of each of the following words and phrases as it is used on the tape.*

1   It was absolutely ludicrous
2   everybody else would have stumbled on it
3   indefinitely
4   in order to convince himself
5   data
6   a minimum stake
7   to hold his hand
8   very sceptical
9   terribly amusing
10   eager
11   aristocratic people
12   it started to build up
13   to drown our sorrows
14   it absolutely cured him
15   it would have actually been his undoing

V   *Write down the five sentences you hear on the tape. Listen very carefully. You will hear each sentence twice.*

VI *Between ten to twelve and twelve o'clock Tom and Tim lost about £300 (although they had £3 left to buy drinks with). They were in France and had to bet in French currency. If the value of their first stake was equivalent, in English currency, to 18p, exactly how much had they lost in total, after doubling their stake ten times?*

It's strange how things seem to happen to some people and how they are always involved in unusual events. Alan is one of those people. Almost unbelievable things have happened to him. When you hear this story you will think, perhaps, that it couldn't possibly be true, but it is.

You will notice that Alan mentions 'a yellow hat'. In fact, it is more accurate to say that a traffic warden's hat is black and yellow.

11 The Silly Story of the Cat

◖I *Listen to this silly story and answer the following questions choosing the right answer from A B C or D.*

1 When Alan drove out of the T-junction he hit
   A a frightful thud
   B nothing
   C somebody walking round
   D an animal

2 Alan went to the butcher's
   A to tell the butcher what had happened
   B to get a bag
   C to ask if the cat belonged to the butcher
   D because he was a cat-lover

3 When Alan got back to the car, after his visit to the butcher's shop, he found out
   A that the cat had gone
   B that he'd got rid of the cat
   C that he'd got a parking ticket
   D how he felt about yellow lines

4 In Alan's opinion, it's not unreasonable to get a parking ticket for parking
   A anywhere in Oxford Street
   B on double yellow lines in Oxford Street
   C in an emergency
   D in a quiet area

5 Alan recognized someone as the traffic warden because
  A she was disappearing round the corner
  B her hat was yellow
  C he looked around
  D he dashed across the street

6 Alan said he wanted the traffic warden to go to his car with him because
  A she'd given him a parking ticket
  B he could explain what had happened and prove it
  C she looked down her nose at him
  D he'd got her by the arm

7 In which of the following places did Alan *not* look for the lost carrier-bag, according to what he says?
  A In the front of the car.   C On the road-way.
  B On the floor.   D By the yellow lines.

8 The woman who was walking off round the corner with a carrier-bag said it wasn't Alan's because
  A it hadn't come from the butcher's
  B she'd been to the butcher's
  C he wasn't the butcher
  D she was crestfallen

9 Alan accused the woman of
  A taking his bag from the butcher's
  B being crestfallen
  C taking the bag from his car
  D proving it was her bag

10 The woman was completely unconscious for some time
  A because Alan shouted at her
  B because she saw what was in the bag
  C because she fainted
  D because she hit her head on the pavement

11 Alan went back to the butcher's shop a second time
   A to call an ambulance   C because the bag had gone
   B to get another bag   D to speak to the traffic warden

II *Now that you have heard Alan's silly story, please answer the following questions.*

1 What did Alan do before driving out at the T-junction?
2 What did Alan intend to do with the carrier-bag he bought from the butcher?
3 What do double yellow lines on the road-side mean?
4 Where is a parking ticket usually left on a car in England?
5 What surprise awaited Alan when he returned to the car with the traffic warden?
6 What did Alan notice about the carrier-bag which he saw a woman carrying away?
7 Exactly what did Alan say to the woman who was carrying a bag from the butcher's?
8 What did the woman do when she saw the dead cat inside the bag she was carrying?
9 Where exactly did Alan leave the woman who had fainted while he tried to get help?
10 Why did Alan go straight home instead of going to work?

III *Listen to Alan describing how he came to hit the cat, and write down exactly what he says.*

IV *Find the following words on the tape and write down the phrase (i.e. the group of words) in which they are spoken, then write an explanation for each phrase.*

1	get over	5	rid of
2	of old	6	emergency
3	thud	7	nose
4	on earth	8	struck

V *Write each of the following in direct speech.*
E.g. Alan told his friends that he thought he'd never get over it.
*   Alan said to his friends, 'I don't think I'll ever get over it.'*

1   George told Alan that he knew the road of old.
2   John remarked that he hoped Alan wasn't a cat-lover.
3   Alan asked at the butcher's if they could sell him a carrier-bag and enquired how much it was.
4   Alan requested the traffic warden to go back to his car with him.
5   Alan accused the woman of having his carrier-bag.
6   Alan accused the woman of having taken the bag from the back of his car.
7   Alan asked the butcher to get an ambulance.

VI *Look at the pictures, and write down what the person indicated might be saying or thinking.*

ALAN (*thinks*): . . . .

ALAN (*thinks*): . . . .

BUTCHER: . . . .

ALAN (*thinks*): . . . .

BUTCHER (*to colleague inside shop*): . . . .

TRAFFIC WARDEN (*thinks*): . . . .

69

12 A Disappointing Holiday for Pam

Holidays are a topic of conversation for months before they happen
and for years afterwards. One remembers particularly holidays that
brought special pleasure or those that turned into disasters. Pam's
story is about a holiday in Switzerland that was not a success. Something seemed to go wrong at every stage through no fault of her own;
she was just unlucky.

 I   *Listen to the story of Pam's disappointing holiday and answer the
following questions by choosing the right answer from* **A B C** *or* **D**.

1   Josephine, who listens to Pam's story,
     A has never been on holiday
     B has been on a skiing holiday and liked it
     C hasn't been on a skiing holiday
     D has been on a skiing holiday and didn't like it

2   When they went shopping for skiing clothes, they did *not* buy
     A ski trousers   **C** sweaters
     B anoraks   **D** boots

3   Pam decided to have lessons because
     A the slopes were dry
     B she was keen
     C her husband encouraged her to
     D she had to go to town three evenings a week

4   They had to wait several hours for their flight because
     A there was fog on the Continent
     B there was fog at Luton
     C the airport was outside London
     D there were no planes going to Wengen

5   Flying to Basle, instead of to Zurich, meant that
    A they could leave Luton earlier
    B they had a longer train journey
    C they had to change flights at Basle
    D they had to wait for a representative in Luton

6   Nicola, Pam's small daughter, was annoyed because
    A people wouldn't answer when she spoke to them
    B the representative didn't come
    C she didn't like television
    D they had missed the train

7   Pam enjoyed the classes in Wengen at first because
    A she had learnt to ski in London
    B no snow fell
    C the snow was fresh
    D the snow was like rock

8   Pam didn't give up in the middle of the lesson on the fourth day,
    although she felt like doing so, because
    A the family wanted her to go on
    B she was so tired that she couldn't think
    C the instructor called her just when she thought she'd stop
    D she fell heavily

9   When Pam had fallen, the instructor
    A told her to get up   C told her she was all right
    B asked if she was all right   D shouted at her

10 When Pam got to hospital, it was decided that
    A she needed an operation
    B she would have to go to another hospital
    C her arm needed setting in a heavy plaster
    D she needed some consolation

II *Now that you've heard about Pam's disappointing holiday, please answer the following questions.*

1. Which members of Pam's family had been on a skiing holiday before?
2. How did the family intend to get skis for their holiday?
3. How long would it have taken Pam to complete her series of skiing lessons in London?
4. What stopped Pam completing the series of lessons in London?
5. Why did they decide to stay in Basle overnight?
6. When did the family arrive in Wengen?
7. Why did the family have to walk from the station at Wengen to their hotel?
8. Which skiing class did Pam join in Wengen?
9. Why did Pam not want to ski on the fourth day?
10. How did Pam hurt her arm?

 III *Find a word or phrase in the story for which each of the following is an explanation.*

1. take part in, play
2. costing a lot of money
3. proved to be
4. water- and wind-proof jackets
5. enthusiastic
6. hurrying
7. accident
8. finally
9. waited around
10. holiday town
11. get cross
12. luggage
13. welcomed
14. smooth and difficult to stand on
15. to continue

IV *In the story, Pam refers to an accident as a 'mishap'. For each of the words or phrases below find a word beginning with 'mis-' which conveys the same meaning. Do not use the same word twice.*

1   put in the wrong place
2   error
3   use wrongly
4   take (something) in a wrong sense
5   behave improperly
6   give wrong information
7   bad luck
8   form a wrong opinion of
9   reckon wrongly
10 doubt the truth or honesty

V *Listen to the extracts from the story and write down the exact words that are said.*

1   'but my husband.......................... and ...., Julie,
    ....'
2   'We, erm, went ....to buy ....' 'And
    expensive, I imagine.' 'Yes, but ....'
3   'My husband said, "...........................? You might ski
    after all." I ...., but he ....,
    so ....lessons. It meant ....
    up to town .... but I ....liked it.'
4   'Well,........................... waiting for .... to come and
    .... nobody came, so we ....
    and went into Basle and, because, er, ...
    we .... to ....the night there.'

VI *Make a list of all the things you would pack for a two-week skiing holiday. You will certainly find 50 things.*

73

13 A Coincidence in New York

Denise went to New York last year to study. She stayed there for five months. In this story, she tells about how she was 'conned' (cheated, tricked) by an old woman one day and about the events that followed.

 I   *Listen to the story and answer the following questions by choosing the right answer from* **A B C** *or* **D.**

1   Denise was sent to room number
    A 1   **C** 100
    B 101   **D** 110

2   Denise had to fill in a form with
    A only the author's name
    B only the title of the book
    C both the author's name and the title of the book
    D her name and the title of the book

3   Denise first met the old woman
    A in the cinema-like room   **C** in the corridor
    B as she left the library   **D** in the original room

4   The old woman said she had come in from the outskirts of
    New York
    A to go to the library   **C** to meet Denise
    B to see a sick friend   **D** to catch the underground train

5   The old woman said that a small piece had been chipped off her
    umbrella
    A by the thief   **C** by the door of the train
    B when she dropped it   **D** when she opened it

6   Denise offered the old woman some money. In fact, in the end
    she gave her
    A two dollars   C twelve dollars
    B ten dollars   D fourteen or fifteen dollars

7   Denise had more money when she got back home than when she
    set out because
    A the old woman had given her ten dollars
    B she had found two dollars
    C someone had given her the wrong change
    D she had collected some money from the bank

8   After waiting for about a week, Denise received
    A half her money   C part of her money
    B all her money   D nothing at all
                                            from the old woman.

9   Denise went into the Barbazon Plaza Hotel one January day
    A for a drink   C to look for the old woman
    B because it was cold outside D to put on her make-up

10 Denise recognized the old woman in the foyer of the hotel
    A by her broken umbrella   C by the feather in her hat
    B by her fur coat   D by her general appearance

II *You have heard Denise's story. Now, please answer the questions*
    below.

1   Why did Denise go to the public library?
2   In what way was the public library in New York different from
    any library Denise had seen before?
3   Why did Denise have to fill in another form?
4   What was it about the old woman's hat which attracted Denise's
    attention?
5   The old woman said that her handbag had been stolen. When did
    this happen, according to her story?

6   What made Denise decide to take the old woman over the road to the tea-shop?
7   Where did Denise leave her handbag while she fetched some tea?
8   Why did the old woman take Denise's address?
9   Why did Denise not retrace her steps when she found more change in her purse than she expected when she got home?
10   Why was it a good idea for Denise to go into the Barbazon Plaza Hotel when she was cold?

III *What did Denise have to do at the public library when she had filled in her form? Listen to the first part of the tape and write* down exactly *what she says, beginning:*
'I was handed a disc . . .
(and ending) I waited and waited and waited!'

IV *Write down the words for the following*

| 101 | 2 | 99 | 20 | 15 |
| 12 | 110 | 10 | 8 | 13 |

V *Copy this form and fill in the details.*

THE CENTRAL LIBRARY		
Name of the borrower	Address of borrower	Date
Author		
Title		
Publisher (if known)		

VI *Denise describes a room in the library as 'cinema-like'. Fill the spaces in the sentences below with adjectives of this type, choosing the most appropriate word from the list below to complete each sentence.*
E.g. *Owl*
Answer: He has an *owl*-like face.

war, church, fish, marble, teacher, child, bear, monkey.

1 There was a . . . . -like smell.
2 It was a . . . . -like building.
3 She gave me a . . . . -like smile.
4 He spoke in a . . . . -like voice.
5 He pulled a . . . . -like face.
6 They did a . . . . -like dance.
7 She had a . . . . -like hand.
8 He gave me a . . . . -like hug.

VII *Now listen to the tape and write down each group of three words in the order in which they are spoken. Listen very carefully! You will hear each set of words twice. There are five questions.*

It is generally thought that an accident is the result of somebody's error or neglect. This tragic incident occurred in spite of Jaeger being a famous balloonist with a great deal of experience and expertise. As a fellow-balloonist, Gerry, who tells the story, is well aware of the skill necessary to inflate a balloon without any help. It is particularly tragic that nobody will ever know exactly what happened.

14 The Tragic Story of the Balloonist

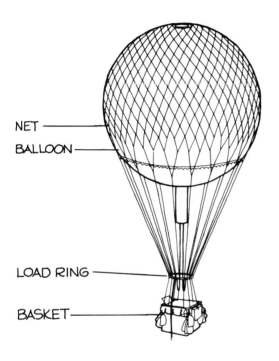

NET
BALLOON
LOAD RING
BASKET

I *Listen to this tragic story told by Gerry and answer the following questions by choosing the right answer from* **A B C** *or* **D**.

1 According to Gerry, Augsberg is a good ballooning centre because
A it's very high
B it's in Germany
C it has fantastic visibility
D waste hydrogen is available there

2   Filling a balloon is hard work because
    A you can't get it near the factory
    B it's very heavy and you must lay it out
    C you must move a ton of sand before you begin
    D you must move 50 sandbags a number of times

3   After about three hours
    A the balloon is beginning to inflate
    B the sandbags are all off the net
    C the balloon is completely inflated
    D the balloon is partly inflated

4   The load-ring is attached
    A to the net only   C to the net and the basket
    B to the balloon only   D to the basket and the balloon

5   This particular balloon would carry
    A 12 people for 3 hours   C 3 people with a struggle
    B 3 people easily for 12 hours   D 12 people for a short time

6   The net gets difficult to handle because
    A it is stiffened by the dew   C it's a calm night
    B it's late in the morning   D dawn breaks

7   When Gerry and his friends went out of the hut, they saw the
    balloon flying off and
    A Jaeger holding the sandbags
    B Jaeger looking at it from the ground
    C Jaeger hanging on to the load-ring
    D Jaeger in the basket

8   The onlookers saw sparks and flashes when
    A the balloon exploded
    B Jaeger, in falling, hit the high-tension wires
    C the balloon hit the high-tension wires
    D Jaeger went into the low cloud

9 Jaeger's wife
A insisted on flying the balloon that killed her husband
B went on ballooning, in the family tradition
C gave up all contacts with ballooning
D said she'd never balloon again, but did

10 It is almost impossible to believe, according to Gerry, that Jaeger
A should have been a balloon-master
B should be dead when they found him
C should have had the same sort of mishap twice and should have been all right the first time but killed the second time
D should have tried again after nearly having the same accident the week before

II *Now that you've heard the tragic story, please answer the following questions.*

1 Why was Herr Jaeger famous, according to Gerry's opening remarks?
2 Where did the hydrogen gas for filling balloons come from?
3 How many people helped Herr Jaeger to fill his balloon?
4 How could Herr Jaeger manage to get the balloon from the hydrogen pipe to the basket?
5 Why did the balloon suddenly start to go up, on the first occasion?
6 Where were Gerry and his friends when they heard a shout and realized something was wrong?
7 Would it have been a good idea for Jaeger to loose and fall to the ground when he had been lifted by the balloon for three seconds?
8 Why could the onlookers never find out exactly what had happened to Jaeger?
9 How do we know that Jaeger's wife knows anything about ballooning?
10 What eventually happened to the balloon, after Jaeger had fallen to the ground?

III *Listen carefully to the story on the tape again and find* twelve *adverbs which end in '-ly' and write them down. Then give an explanation for each one as it is used on the tape.*
E.g. Carefully (not on tape): *with care.*

IV *Listen to your tape and write down the groups of three words which you hear. Listen very carefully. You will hear each group of words twice. There are twenty groups.*

V *Gerry uses a number of technical terms for ballooning:* balloon, net, load-ring, basket. *Here are some words associated with particular sports. For each group find the sport.*

1   ball, pitch, penalty area, goal
2   boots, snow, slope, slalom
3   racket, deuce, service, back-hand
4   chequered flag, track, tyres, mechanic
5   water, stroke, dive, starter
6   ice, figures, blade, jumps
7   spikes, starting-blocks, tape, lane
8   jockey, colours, saddle, paddock
9   puck, penalty-box, red line, blue line
10 pedals, wheel, handle-bars, saddle

VI *Below are some illustrations which help a would-be balloonist to understand how to inflate a balloon. Write a title for each picture.*

15 The Unfortunate Story of the Lost Money

Tom's story is about an unfortunate situation which he was unable to put right in the end. It shows how careful one should be about making accusations. You may think that Tom should be criticized for making a hasty decision and for not being prepared to reconsider it later. Or you may feel that the whole story was 'just one of those unfortunate things'. 'Quid' is a slang term for 'pound' or 'pounds'.

 I *Listen to Tom's unfortunate story and answer the following questions by choosing the right answer from* **A B C** *or* **D**.

1   Tom
   A had had a cook for three months
   B had been on leave for several weeks
   C had been in that place for several years
   D had just been on leave to England

2   In the time that Tom was going to be away, Idris, the cook
   A was going to get everything ready
   B was going to go away too
   C would have a lot of things to do
   D was going to stay there

3   Tom took a lot of money out of the bank because
   A he needed to pay Idris
   B he needed the money to take to England
   C he had some bills to pay
   D he wanted to fix up the house

4 All the rooms in Tom's house led
   A to his bedroom   C to passages in the house
   B to each other   D to the veranda

5 Having realized that the money had disappeared, Tom went to
   Idris's room
   A to search it   C to see if he'd gone out
   B to get the keys   D because it was locked

6 The police refused to go and investigate whether Idris had stolen
   the money unless
   A he sorted it out
   B Tom made an accusation against Idris
   C Tom really suspected Idris
   D Tom went back to the police station

7 Tom didn't want to make a definite accusation that Idris had
   taken the money
   A because he didn't have any evidence
   B because he was suspicious
   C because of the circumstances
   D because he felt desperate

8 When Tom told Idris that he didn't trust him any more and that
   he was sacking him, Idris's first reaction was to
   A shrug his shoulders   C get very angry
   B promise to return the money D cry

9 Tom gave Osman some old magazines because
   A Idris had left   C Tom was finally going home
   B Tom was going on holiday D Osman had come back

10 Tom thought that
   A Osman's finding the money C he, himself,
   B Idris   D the whole affair
                                  was 'pretty unfortunate'.

85

II *Now answer these questions about the story you have heard, please.*

1 Where did Tom have this unfortunate experience?
2 Why was Tom going to close the house up?
3 Where, exactly, did Tom put the £65 which he took out of the bank?
4 Why did Tom want the money next morning?
5 What was Tom's first thought when he realized the money had gone?
6 Why did Tom feel guilty when he went to Idris's room?
7 What did Tom ask the police to do?
8 How did Idris behave when Tom first mentioned the disappearance of the money to him?
9 What did Tom give to Idris on the day he left? Why did he give him this?
10 What is *Encounter*?

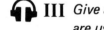 **III** *Give an explanation of the following words and phrases as they are used in the story.*

1 he was going to go off
2 to fix up
3 clearing up
4 without showing some sort of sign of entry
5 he had access to all the keys
6 searched the room
7 my cook, whom I suspected
8 made a definite accusation
9 he didn't register anything
10 I let it drift
11 he absolutely went through the roof
12 a friend dropped in
13 in lieu of notice

IV *Tom says that, 'being a coward', he didn't sack Idris immediately.*
Complete the following sentences using the expression 'being a ...'

1   Being a . . . . . . , he played beautiful music.
2   Being a . . . . . . , he did lots of experiments.
3   Being a . . . . . . , he told the students what to do.
4   Being an . . . . . . , he can do the job very well.
5   Being a . . . . . . , he was able to repair the car immediately.
6   Being a . . . . . . , she was met by vast numbers of reporters and cameramen.
7   Being a . . . . . . , he got everything wrong.
8   Being a . . . . . . , he has made a fortune.

V *Listen to Exercise V on your tape. You will hear what Tom says at the end of the story. Write down his exact words. You will need to stop the tape to give yourself time to write.*

VI *Find phrases from the tape which express ideas of place and use each one in an appropriate space below (being sure to include the correct preposition), so that they complete the sentences sensibly. You may only use exact phrases from the tape.*

1   He's lived . . . . for years.
2   I want to go . . . . for my holiday this year.
3   Let's draw some money . . . .
4   Leave the paper . . . . of the desk.
5   She went . . . . to sit in the sun.
6   The window of my hotel faced . . . .
7   He wanted a policeman, so he went . . . .
8   It's time for lunch; let's go . . . .
9   I've hidden your wallet. . . . .
10   You'll find that money . . . . you're reading now.

16 A Worrying Evening Waiting for News

Uncertainty was Elizabeth's problem. She didn't know whether the worst had happened or not and she had great difficulty in finding out.

In this story, Elizabeth refers to BEA, British European Airways, which has since become part of British Airways Corporation. She uses a number of phrases associated with travel, such as 'checked-in', 'take off', 'flight number' and 'passenger list'.

You will notice that Carol mentions Tony's brother, but in fact only Elizabeth's brother was involved in this story and Carol had made a mistake.

I *Listen to Elizabeth's worrying story and answer the following questions by choosing the right answer from A B C or D.*

1 On the Sunday when her husband, Tony, was going to Brussels, Elizabeth
   A drove him to the airport with her daughter
   B drove him to the airport bus terminal
   C stayed at home with her small daughter
   D drove him to the airport alone

2 The first phone call Elizabeth received when she got home from the airport was from
   A the airport   C her husband's father
   B her father   D her husband

3   Elizabeth first realized that the crash she had heard about on the radio might be something to do with her when
    A she heard a second radio bulletin
    B she panicked
    C she realized it was eight o'clock
    D her brother telephoned

4   Elizabeth's brother phoned to tell her
    A there had not been a plane crash
    B her husband was still at the airport
    C her husband was not on the plane that had crashed
    D her husband was on the plane that had crashed

5   Elizabeth
    A hadn't seen her husband's ticket and didn't know the flight number
    B hadn't seen her husband's ticket but knew the flight number
    C had seen her husband's ticket and knew the flight number
    D had seen her husband's ticket but didn't know the flight numbe

6   The television news later in the evening reported that the plane had taken off
    A within an hour of five o'clock
    B at 5.20 p.m.
    C within an hour of six o'clock
    D at 6.10 p.m.

7   When Elizabeth's brother rang the airline, they would not
    A give him any information
    B answer the phone
    C give names of passengers on other flights
    D confirm or deny whether someone was on the crashed plane

8   The airline did not have a complete passenger list because
    A it was on the crashed plane
    B block bookings had been made by agents

C they never have passenger lists
D lists are always terrible

9 Elizabeth only really finally believed that Tony wasn't on the
crashed plane when
A he phoned her that night   C he came home three days later
B he phoned her next day   D he phoned her three days later

10 After this experience, Elizabeth
A still feels equally confident about air travel
B is less worried than she used to be about air travel
C is a little more anxious about air travel
D will never go on a plane again

II *Now that you have heard Elizabeth's story, please answer the
questions below.*

1 Why was Elizabeth's husband, Tony, going to catch a plane?
2 Had Tony ever gone away by plane before?
3 What was Elizabeth doing when the telephone rang the first time?
4 What words exactly did Elizabeth hear when she put the radio on?
5 Did the phone call from her brother help Elizabeth to understand
what had happened?
6 What gave Elizabeth the impression that Tony had gone on a BEA
plane?
7 Elizabeth remembered that Tony had told her the time he
expected to take off. What time did she think he had said?
8 What information, which Elizabeth suggests would have helped
her to know whether it was Tony's flight or not, was not given on
the news?
9 Who rang the airline to get information for Elizabeth?
10 At what time was information finally given about the take-off
time of the crashed plane?

III *Elizabeth considers her experience 'unfortunate'. For each of the following words or phrases below, find a word beginning with 'un-' which conveys the same meaning.*

1 take off one's clothes
2 not sure to happen
3 prohibited by law
4 single (of a person)
5 disagreeable
6 not friendly
7 dangerous
8 without the necessary qualifications
9 nervous
10 intolerable

 IV *Find a word or phrase in the story for which each of the following is an explanation.*

1 concerned
2 often
3 unhappy
4 turned on
5 decided from what I heard
6 announcement
7 condition
8 remembered
9 certainly
10 made things clear

V *Below are some expressions which Elizabeth uses in telling her story. Use each one as the beginning of a short sentence of your own.*

1 On the Sunday ...

2   No, no, no, no ...
3   Could I ...
4   As I switched on ...
5   I concluded ...
6   At that point ...
7   The next thing I knew ...
8   All he said was ...
9   By that time ...
10 In other words ...
11 Within an hour of ...
12 Had we known ...
13 They were only prepared . .
14 In the end ...
15 Though I was never worried ...

VI *Find every time mentioned in the story and write down briefly what happened at that time. (You should find eight specific times mentioned.)*

17 An Amusing Day on a Building Site

When Ricky was a student, he worked as a labourer on a building site during his Easter vacation. He wanted to save some money to pay for his summer holidays. Although he had to work very hard, he had many funny adventures. This is the story of one of his most amusing days when he was supposed to deliver wheelbarrow loads of liquid concrete to a skilled workman.

Ricky sometimes uses the word 'cement' when he means 'concrete'. Cement is the dry powder which is mixed with sand, stones and water to make concrete.

I *Listen to the story and answer the following questions by choosing the right answer from A B C or D.*

1   Ricky worked on a building site
    A every holiday when he was a student
    B all the time
    C for two Easter holidays in consecutive years
    D for two years

2   The 'gangers' mentioned in the story were
    A head waiters   C Irish waiters
    B head labourers   D hard men

3   Ricky describes 'hard men' as
    A 'chaps who reckon they're terrifically tough'
    B 'chaps who are gangers'
    C 'chaps who call themselves hard men'
    D 'chaps who are Irish'

4   Ricky had to wheel the wheelbarrow quite fast along the planks
     because
     A the boss had told him to
     B he would have fallen off the planks if he had gone slowly
     C he had to be able to bump off the end of one plank on to the
        next one
     D he had to move quickly through the water

5   Ricky was expected to tip the liquid concrete
     A on to the plank   C into the deep hole
     B on to the plywood   D on to the side of the hole

6   When Ricky attempted to tip the liquid concrete
     A he fell into the wheelbarrow
     B the wheelbarrow and concrete fell into the hole
     C the concrete fell out of the wheelbarrow on to the plywood
     D the wheelbarrow, the concrete and Ricky fell into the hole

7   The 'hard man' on the site was
     A quite young but not friendly   C unfriendly
     B old and friendly   D quite young and quite friendly

8   The 'hard man' said to Ricky
     A 'Here, I'll show you how to do it'
     B 'Now, I'll show you how to do it'
     C 'Here, show me how to do it'
     D 'Here, now show me how to do it'

9   When the 'hard man' reached the edge of the hole
     A he stopped
     B he tipped the concrete on to the edge of the hole
     C the wheelbarrow and the concrete fell into the hole
     D the man fell into the hole

10 When the Irishman down the hole had been covered with concrete
    for the second time
    A he shouted at the two men
    B he disappeared down the sump
    C he disappeared out of the gate and never came back
    D he disappeared out of the gate and came back the next day

II *You have listened to Ricky's story, now answer the following
    questions, please.*

1   What did Ricky find particularly difficult to do when he was
    working as a labourer on a building site?
2   What sort of load makes the planks sag a lot when the barrow is
    wheeled over them?
3   What did Ricky find he worried about as he moved along the
    plank with the barrow?
4   What was the purpose of the extra deep hole, which Ricky called
    'a kind of sump', in the corner of the main hole where the man
    waited to spread the concrete?
5   What did Ricky see when he looked over the edge of the hole
    after the concrete had spilled into the sump?
6   Did Ricky think the 'hard man' who offered to demonstrate how
    to wheel and tip the barrow was really good at the job?
7   Why did the 'hard man's' hair stream back as he wheeled the
    barrow across the planks?
8   What had the Irishman in the hole just done when the second
    load of concrete tipped over him?
9   What did the two men see when they first looked over the side
    of the hole?
10 What did the Irishman do when he had been covered with concrete
    for the second time and before he climbed out of the hole?

III *Here are some of the words from the story. Use each one in a sentence to show that you have understood the meaning of the word.*

1   planks   6   slid
2   overlap   7   splashed
3   sags   8   statue
4   enable   9   shovel
5   accurately   10   dumbfounded

IV *Some colloquial phrases are used in the story. Write another phrase of similar meaning to each of the following as they are used in the story.*

1   You hare along
2   It whips up
3   I got the knack
4   I made it
5   He charged over the planks

V *Write down the five sentences that you hear spoken on the tape. Listen very carefully! You will hear each sentence twice.*

VI *For this exercise you will hear a single word, which will be said twice. Choose the answer which best explains the word.*

1   **A** the place where you live
     B hollow place
     C small mountain
     D large room for meetings and concerts

2   **A** stay where one is   **C** not dry
     B move the hand to and fro   **D** left

98

3   A border
    B boundary formed by bushes
    C length of time a person has lived
    D top section of the body

4   A put out of sight
    B almost fall because of taking a false step
    C move very smoothly
    D expresses pleasure

5   A fellow   C small animal
    B costing little money   D cut with an axe

6   A disagreeably bright
    B person who tells lies
    C unusual
    D a horizontal piece (usually one is put on top of another)

18 The Horrifying Happenings at a Student Demonstration

To find oneself in the midst of an angry crowd is unpleasant enough, but Liz saw the crowd shocked and frightened by the events that occurred and she found this a horrifying experience.

In this story, you will hear the rather unusual word 'pall', meaning the cloth (usually black or purple) put over a coffin.

 I *Listen to this horrifying story and answer the following questions by choosing the right answer from A B C or D.*

1 All the students in the country were very angry because
A they didn't know what had happened
B they didn't like the President of the Students' Union
C the President of the country had been killed
D a student had been killed

2 Liz, the university teacher, mentions three groups of people who came to join in the protest march. Which of the following are *not* mentioned?
A university students   C college students
B university teachers   D children from schools

3 Liz was very tired because
A she was going away for the week-end
B she had been marking examinations
C she was oblivious of what was happening
D she walked to the garage

4   Liz didn't really realize there was anything wrong until
     A she got to the garage
     B she saw the crowd in the town
     C she found herself standing near the coffin in the middle of a
        police cordon
     D she spoke to a policeman

5   Liz went to hide behind the fence because
     A the police told her to
     B she knew the people there
     C a waitress called to her to do so
     D some students suggested that she should

6   After she had gone into the grounds of the café, Liz knew what
     was going on because
     A a waitress described the scene to her
     B she looked through the window
     C she looked over the gate
     D she looked through a hole in the fence

7   The armoured trucks arrived
     A to collect the coffin
     B to take the police away
     C to collect the students who were following the coffin
     D to bring more police to the scene

8   The body of the dead student had been
     A taken by the police   C hidden by the students
     B taken away by his parents   D buried earlier by the students

9   The funeral procession and demonstration went on without the
     body because
     A nobody knew there was no body
     B the students wanted the opportunity to demonstrate
     C the police thought it would be safer to go ahead
     D the parents of the boy wanted it to

10   The police got to know that there was no body in the coffin
     A from the parents   C from an informer
     B from the university students D from the army

II *Now that you have heard the story, please answer the following questions.*

1   Who had been killed in a riot?
2   How did the students intend to show their anger about the death?
3   Where was the coffin kept until the day of the funeral?
4   Why did Liz, the university teacher, need to go to the garage?
5   How far away was the garage from Liz's house?
6   How does Liz describe the atmosphere when she realized that the situation in the town was dangerous?
7   What did the police officer do after he had taken the black cloth off the coffin?
8   What fact caused the crowd to gasp in horror?
9   What sort of comments passed among the crowd after they realized the truth about the coffin?
10   Where, in fact, was the student going to be buried?

III *Find a word or phrase in the story for which each of the following is an explanation.*
E.g. made up their minds.   Answer: *decided*

1   in the grounds of the university
2   to collect (my car)
3   unaware
4   very anxious
5   something that happens
6   called to me
7   looked
8   walked with big strides
9   the black cloth

102

10 to pull roughly
11 taken for granted
12 moving in a confused way
13 a low noise
14 prevented from having
15 unpleasant

IV *Listen to Exercise IV on your tape. You will hear a part of the story. Write down the exact words spoken by Liz.*

V *Here are some words from the story. Find another word (not necessarily from the story) to rhyme with each one.*
E.g. sad. Answer: bad

1	riot	11	quick
2	march	12	trouble
3	car	13	strode
4	tired	14	wrench
5	streets	15	killed
6	crowd	16	fighting
7	through	17	trucks
8	round	18	drove
9	thought	19	bury
10	tense	20	chance

VI *Imagine this story being reported in the newspapers. Think of six possible headlines it could be given and write down each one. (A headline is usually not more than 6 or 7 words).*

19 The Dramatic Events at the Bank

This dramatic story caused great excitement to all who followed it, but because few got really first-hand details at the time, the account which Ingrid and David give to their friends is a little complicated. In their excitement, Ingrid and David get slightly confused about who was shot in the hand when the police entered the bank. In fact, it was the gunman who shot a policeman.

The gunman demanded that a car should be available for him to use for his getaway. The car put outside the bank for this purpose was a Mustang.

I *Listen to this dramatic story and answer the following questions by choosing the right answer from* **A B C** *or* **D**.

1 The drama at the bank started
   A yesterday   C on a Thursday
   B on a Tuesday   D on a Sunday

2 The robber took six hostages. They were
   A people who worked in the bank
   B policemen
   C customers
   D passers-by

3 After three out of the six hostages had been freed, four were still being held! This was because
   A someone miscounted at the beginning
   B one of the three who were free to go didn't do so

C the robber found a man hiding in the bank

D the wounded policeman was being held too

4 The gunman wasn't pleased when he got the money, not only because he only got half the amount he wanted, but also because

A he hadn't got the prisoner

B it was in unused notes

C it was in another currency

D he didn't get it on the day he asked for it

5 The drugged sandwiches did not have the desired effect on the gunman because

A he didn't like bread and so didn't eat them

B the policeman ate them all himself

C the policeman refused to eat them and so the gunman realized they were a trick

D it was a stupid idea

6 When they moved into the vault, they had enough food for two days because

A the police gave them two days' rations

B the man from prison had brought food with him

C there was always enough food for two days kept in the vault

D they had kept some of the food delivered to them earlier

7 The police would only agree to the gunman and his friend leaving if they

A didn't take the Mustang

B took all the hostages with them

C left all the hostages behind

D only took two hostages with them

8 The gunman prevented the police from using tear-gas by

A standing the hostages under the holes

B blocking the holes

C tying his hostages together

D putting a noose round each hostage's neck

9   The second attempt to put tear-gas in through the roof was to be
    accompanied by
    A   policemen speaking to the men by radio
    B   people trying to find a new plan
    C   two volunteer policemen trying to get in through the vault door
    D   two civilian volunteers going into the bank

10 At the time of the telling of the story, the gunman was
    A   in the vault
    B   in hospital, recovering
    C   in prison, having been found guilty
    D   still being questioned

II *Now that you have heard the dramatic story, please answer the
    following questions.*

1   How many people went to rob the bank?
2   The man made two demands when he had taken his hostages.
    What were these demands?
3   When the prisoner was brought to the bank, three hostages were let
    free. How does Ingrid describe these three?
4   How do we know that there wasn't a huge crowd all around the
    bank watching what was going on?
5   Where did the gunman and his friend and the hostages go after
    three days?
6   Were the hostages men or women?
7   How did the police plan to get tear-gas into the vault?
8   What clever scheme did the gunman devise to prevent the police
    using tear-gas at first?
9   How did the gunman know what the police were planning outside
    the vault?
10 Was the prisoner who had been released taken back to his prison
    cell immediately?

III *Find a word or phrase in the story for which each of the following is an explanation.*

E.g. hurrying   Answer: *rushing*

1	a request	10	bored and tired of waiting
2	released from (prison)	11	situation
3	a clever scheme	12	drilled
4	to force people to do things	13	a loop of rope
5	expecting a baby	14	clever thinking
6	to go on for	15	precisely
7	quantity	16	intelligence
8	holding discussions	17	surrendered
9	silly	18	interrogated

IV *Complete the ten sentences below by using a word from the following list.*

vandals	blackmailers	shoplifters	murderers
criminals	smugglers	kidnappers	terrorists
bank robbers	drug addicts	arsonists	
stowaways	traitors		

E.g. People who commit crimes are called ....
    Answer: *criminals*

1   People who take things from shops without paying for them are called ....

2   People who steal money from banks are called ....

3   People who betray their country are called ....

4   People who take things into a country illegally are called ....

5   People who take drugs in excess, not for medical reasons, are called ....

6   People who smash public buildings and other people's property are called ....

7   People who set fire to other people's property are called ....

8   People who hide on ships in order to travel without paying are called ....

9   People who demand money in exchange for keeping secrets are called ....
10   People who detain others against their will and demand ransom money for their release are called ....

V   *In England, if you want money, you go to the bank. Complete the following sentences (remembering that they are all concerned with England).*

1   If you want to buy stamps, you go to the ....
2   If you want to book a holiday, you go to the ....
3   If you want to see a film, you go to the ....
4   If you want to get your car repaired, you go to the ....
5   If you want to get your hair cut, you go to the ....
6   If you want to have a glass of beer, you go to the ....
7   If you want to get your clothes washed, you go to the ....
8   If you want to catch a train, you go to the ....
9   If you want to get on a bus, you go to the ....
10   If you want to see a play, you go to the ....

VI   *Imagine that you were in charge of keeping the police record of what happened each day during the gunman's occupation of the bank. Write down the daily diary in very brief note form. (You will find some days mentioned in the story. The rest you must make up for yourself.)*
Begin:
Tuesday: gunman entered bank

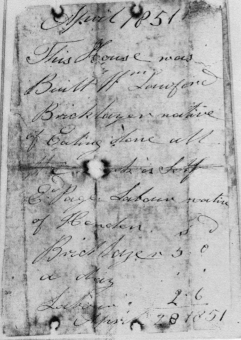

20 The Fascinating Story of a Find in the Roof

In this story, Michael says he telephoned the Victoria and Albert Museum. This would be the usual way for a person living in London to get the sort of information he wanted.

Michael also mentions 'a promising little company called ICI'. Imperial Chemical Industries is now a large international company, but Michael imagines that in 1851 the occupants of the house might have left him shares in that company which would, a hundred years later, be worth a fortune.

The rates of pay for the workman in 1851 are listed as 5/- (five shillings) a day and 2/6d (two shillings and sixpence) a day, which is equivalent to 25p and 12½p in the decimal currency of today.

Michael still lives in the house where he found the 'curious thing' and now one almost expects him to discover other fascinating objects.

I *Listen to Michael's fascinating story and answer the following questions by choosing the right answer from A B C or D.*

1 The centre part of the house is
   A older   C bigger
   B newer   D smaller
   than the rest of the house.

2 Michael got experts to help him
   A to knock walls down
   B to dig floors up
   C to do goodness knows what
   D to do the things he didn't understand

3   The plumbing in the house
    A had been replaced exactly 100 years before
    B needed replacing
    C had been replaced by craftsmen
    D had to be replaced by a water-tank

4   Michael had to take a vacuum cleaner into the roof because
    A nobody had been there before
    B the house was very old
    C the dust was very thick
    D he wanted to get the water-tank in

5   When Michael first saw the 'curious object', it was
    A on the water-tank   C in the hole in the ceiling
    B wired up to the light   D nailed to a beam

6   The envelope seemed more interesting to Michael when he
    realized
    A it had a red seal on it   C it was covered in dust
    B it was small   D it was ginger

7   The envelope began to fall apart when Michael touched it because
    A it had writing on it
    B it had been there so long
    C Michael tried to tear it open
    D Michael had spoilt it as he took it down

8   The expert at the Victoria and Albert Museum said that the
    envelope was too fragile to open and would
    A need to be kept dry for some days
    B not last very long
    C have to be soaked in a special solution
    D have to be opened by another expert

9   The envelope contained another envelope which contained
     A a treasure map   C a red seal
     B shares in a company   D a letter

10   Michael intends to
     A put the original letter back in the roof pretending he has never
        seen it
     B give the letter to the Victoria and Albert Museum
     C photograph the letter and put the photograph and a letter of
        explanation in the roof
     D explain how he found the letter to his children who will tell
        the next occupants of the house

II   *Now that you have heard Michael's fascinating story, please
     answer the following questions.*

1   What is unusual about the building which Michael bought about
     three years ago?
2   Why did Michael begin to do major alterations on the house
     about a year ago?
3   Why did Michael have to cut a hole in the ceiling?
4   Why did Michael put a fluorescent light in the roof?
5   What did Michael do to 'the curious object' when he first saw it?
6   What, approximately, were the dimensions of the envelope?
7   Exactly what was written on the envelope?
8   What did Michael do with the envelope to protect it?
9   What would the effect of soaking the envelope be, according to
     the expert at the Museum?
10   Who had written the letter in the envelope?

III *Michael and Mary discuss what he might have found in the
     envelope. Find that part of the story on the tape (about half way
     through) and list the four possibilities mentioned. Then add five
     more possibilities of things which you think he could have found.*

IV *Use the following words and phrases in sentences of your own to show that you have understood their meaning in the story.*

1	knocked together	8	beams
2	much more recent	9	gingerly
3	modify	10	exquisite copper-plate writing
4	craftsmen	11	contained my impatience
5	replaced	12	a treasure map
6	wired up	13	restore
7	peak	14	fascinating

V *Find a word which rhymes with each of the words below and then give an explanation of the word you find. If you are not sure about the sound of a word in the list, you can find it on the tape.*

E.g. house   Answer: *mouse (small animal)*

1	knocked	6	roof
2	recent	7	dust
3	needs	8	nailed
4	dig	9	seal
5	plumbing	10	prize

VI *Using the pictures of the letter on page 110 and Michael's reading of the letter on the tape, write the workmen's letter in the language it would be written in today.*

Answers

1   THE LUCKY STORY OF THE HOLIDAY MONEY

I   1 C   3 C   5 C   7 C   9 B
         2 B   4 D   6 D   8 A   10 D

II   1   They went *to Italy and France.*
         2   She put all the money and documents in a folder because
              they *had had an awful lot of trouble finding the passports*
              and other documents *at the border.*
         3   She put *the passports, the tickets, the travellers' cheques*
              and *all* their *currency* into a folder.
         4   The *real* reason was *to ask the way to the camp-site.*
         5   To try and find the folder, they took *everything out of the
              car.*
         6   They went *back to the town* to *go to the police station.*
         7   They went *back to the garage* because they *suddenly* thought
              that somebody at the garage must have stolen their *folder.*
         8   They *persuaded her by asking her to give* them *directions* to
              somewhere, *and she stood up to speak* to them.
         9   The good news was that *someone* had *found* their *folder* and
              phoned the camp-site to say so.
         10   They realized that it was *going to the camp-site* because it
              was loaded with a *tent and camping* gear and going up *a
              country lane* towards the site.

2   THE MYSTERIOUS EVENTS AT A COUNTRY HOUSE

I   1 D   3 B   5 B   7 A   9 B
         2 C   4 B   6 C   8 B   10 D

II   1   No, she doesn't.
         2   No, she isn't. She *would be more impressed by something
              that happened to* Brian himself.

3   The big house was *about ten miles from the coast.*

4   They thought *thieves* might go to the house.

5   It was *up a long drive, surrounded by fir trees* (and *away from the village*).

6   She was *watching television.*

7   His appearance made her think he was a business man. He was a *respectable, elderly man* wearing *a dark suit, a smart tie, and a bowler hat and* he *was carrying a brief-case.*

8   *She said 'Good evening! Can I help you?'*

9   He said that he had *something important to tell her.*

10   *She said, 'My father? Don't be silly! My father's been dead for fifteen years.'*

3   THE HAPPY STORY OF A TRAMP

I   1 B   3 A   5 C   7 C   9 C
        2 C   4 D   6 C   8 D   10 B

II   1   His circle became smaller *as he got older and his feet* became *very bad.*

2   She gave him *meals, clothing,* and *a few shillings.*

3   He thought Mr Rutley should be receiving a pension because *he was getting on for seventy.*

4   They gave him *little cakes, biscuits,* and other things they had cooked.

5   They *washed cars, gave their pocket money, did odd jobs,* and collected money from the parents who came to see their *production of 'The Mikado'.*

6   He calls it a *'shepherd's hut'.*

7   *He towed it* on *a tractor.*

8   She mentions *bed, bedding, cutlery and crockery.*

9   *The only thing* they *hadn't got was a cooker.*

10   He collects his *pension and his groceries* from the village and *milk and bread* from the school.

4 THE FRIGHTENING CONSEQUENCES OF FINDING A BODY

I 1 C   3 D   5 B   7 C   9 D
   2 B   4 D   6 D   8 A   10 A

II 1 It began at *three* o'clock in the morning.
   2 She decided they were not about to be ambushed when she realized they were in *open country* with *no bushes* or other *cover* at the roadside where robbers could hide.
   3 No, she wasn't alone. She *had a friend* called *Michael* with her.
   4 It was difficult because he was *heavy* and *unconscious* and they *didn't want to hurt him.*
   5 It wasn't possible to ask the man what had happened because he *died* next day without regaining *consciousness.*
   6 She mentions that they wanted to know, for example, *the angle* at which *the body was lying* and *whether it was facing north or south.*
   7 They said she had *knocked* the *man down* and then run *over him several times.*
   8 She was charged with *capital murder.*
   9 She *went in the Embassy lorry with the Vice-Consul and the* Embassy *guards.*
   10 *The girls in the bar* where the *fight* had started had told *the police.*

5 AN EMBARRASSING MOMENT FOR JOHN

I 1 A   3 A   5 C   7 B   9 B
   2 C   4 A   6 B   8 D   10 D

II 1 She lived on *the fifth floor of a block of flats in* a *part of Stockholm.*
   2 He came home between *eleven o'clock and midnight.*
   3 The man *had a coat on and a hat in his hand.*
   4 He *got out on the fifth floor.*

5　He didn't send it back to the ground floor because he thought that the man and woman *would call it back to the fourth floor* for the man to get in and leave.

6　John hoped that the man would think he had gone into a flat and so would get into the lift and leave.

7　He had to hop because one of his ankles made a noise when he walked.

8　He said he *felt like a trapped animal.*

9　He wanted him to see that he was going to his own flat on the fourth floor.

10　He said *'Goodnight'.*

6　THE SAD LIFE OF AN OLD MAN

I　1 C　　3 B　　5 D　　7 C　　9 A
　　2 C　　4 B　　6 B　　8 C　　10 D

II　1　The *survey* was about *the needs of disabled people in the borough.*

2　She says they were *quite poor, lived in very bad housing conditions, tended to be elderly and had some quite bad disabilities.*

3　*He grumbled about young people, the rising cost of living, the government and about how the area had gone down.*

4　She went *back to* her *office* and *wrote up the interview.*

5　Yes, he was. His *family* was *quite well-to-do but not spectacularly rich.*

6　He began to support them when his parents *died* and *he took over the* family grocery *business.*

7　*One sister got married* and *the other emigrated* to Australia.

8　He developed arthritis as he got older.

9　He was considered *powerful*, he was *respected* and he was looked on as *somebody of note in the area.*

10　He was *old, frail, in pain* and *he'd lost everything.*

7   AN UNCOMFORTABLE SITUATION FOR BRIAN

I   1 A   3 B   5 D   7 D   9 B   11 C
2 D   4 C   6 B   8 C   10 D

II   1   He was to lecture on *how to use an overhead projector* and on *how to use the language laboratory.*
2   He expected him to *read, rest and watch television.*
3   He lived in the *top flat* of a *block down the road* from the school.
4   He *felt* particularly *uncomfortable because all the furniture was piled up.*
5   Brian thought his friend was *either spring-cleaning* or preparing *to go away on holiday.*
6   He saw *books on biology, chemistry and botany.*
7   He sat on the *corner of the sofa.*
8   No, he *didn't.*
9   He was disinclined to walk *round Brighton* because *it was raining.*
10 *The dog* wasn't in the flat because Mr Brooks had taken it to *the school* for *the day.*

8   AN ALARMING EXPERIENCE ON THE ROAD

I   1 D   3 C   5 D   7 A   9 B
2 C   4 B   6 B   8 B   10 C

II   1   They were *driving to Norwich* because they both *teach there.*
2   John saw *the driver* of the Lotus *slump over the wheel.*
3   John's *friend* walked *on the grass verge* and John walked *in the road.*
4   It hit John's *car.*
5   It finally stopped *in the thick part of* a *hedge* further down the road.

6   *Grass* and *mud* were being thrown *all over the road* by *the back wheels* of the Lotus which were spinning because the engine was still running and the accelerator *was still* being pressed.

7   They also *turned the ignition off.*

8   He got *blankets from people* who *had stopped* near the accident.

9   He was given *a breathalyser test* to check whether he had had too much to drink, as the police thought he *had been driving* his *car* at the time of the crash.

10   The news that *the man* in the Lotus *was dead* was phoned in to the police station.

9   A REMARKABLE EVENT CAUSED BY THE WIND

I   1 A   3 D   5 B   7 A   9 B
      2 C   4 C   6 C   8 C   10 D

II   1   Gerry's daughter *is the only girl in England, and at one stage was the only girl in the world,* to hold *private pilots' licences for hot-air balloons, gas-filled balloons and light aircraft.*

      2   When *using a Humpty Dumpty balloon,* one *jumps* and *floats into the air,* and then one *lands* and *repeats the procedure.*

      3   He introduced the sport of using a Humpty Dumpty balloon and bouncing across the countryside.

      4   They went there because *she was going to do a film sequence for 'Magpie'.*

      5   They wanted her to do *a little lift-off so* that *they could position their cameras.*

      6   At the moment when Christine *was coming down to the ground, there was a tremendous gust of wind.*

      7   Christine was *forty feet below the balloon.*

      8   She *fell on to a path* beside the studio wall.

      9   He found that she was alive, *just conscious and breathing.*

      10   *Her skull was protected* by *her* crash *helmet.*

10   A MORAL LEARNT IN FRANCE

I   1 D   3 C   5 C   7 B   9 A
      2 A   4 B   6 D   8 D   10 C

II 1 He thought that one should *double up on red or on black until it came up.* (In other words, he thought that a player should double the amount of money he bet on a colour at each spin).

2 Tom was going to get *one-third of the winnings.*

3 They went by *air ferry.*

4 *Six* people travelled on the plane.

5 They got on the road first because they *got through customs faster than* the other people did.

6 *The Marquis of Bath and his wife and Lord and Lady Manchester* were at the casino.

7 They agreed to *stop at twelve o'clock.*

8 They lost all their money by doubling *on red or black ten times in ten minutes.*

9 They *burned them all* on a little bonfire which they lit *in the wood* on their way home from the casino.

10 It was a good thing that they lost the money because *if Tim had won it would have been* the beginning of a gambling life for him.

11   THE SILLY STORY OF THE CAT

I   1 D   3 C   5 B   7 A   9 C   11 A
      2 B   4 B   6 B   8 B   10 D

II 1 He *stopped* and *looked left and right* to check that *the road was clear.*

2 He intended *to put the* dead *cat in the carrier-bag and get rid of it somehow.*

3 They mean that it is an area in which one is not allowed to park.

4   It's usually left under *the windscreen-wiper.*

5   The *carrier-bag had gone.*

6   He *noticed* that her *carrier-bag* had *the butcher's name* on it.

7   He said: *'You've got my carrier-bag'.*

8   When she saw the dead cat, *she fainted, fell to the ground and knocked herself out* by striking *her head on the pavement.*

9   He left the woman *lying in the gutter.*

10   He went straight home because he'd had enough for that day.

12   A DISAPPOINTING HOLIDAY FOR PAM

I   1 C   3 C   5 B   7 C   9 B
         2 D   4 A   6 A   8 C   10 C

II   1   Her *husband and* her *elder daughter, Julie, had* both *been* on a skiing holiday *before.*

2   They intended *to hire* them.

3   It would have taken her four weeks.

4   She *got 'flu.*

5   They *decided to stay* in *Basle* overnight because they had *missed the train* to Wengen and they had their *two-and-a-half year old* daughter with them.

6   They arrived *at lunch-time* on *the day* after they had flown to Basle.

7   They had to walk because *there* were *no cars* in Wengen.

8   She joined *the beginners' class.*

9   She didn't want to ski because she was feeling *tired.*

10   She hurt her arm by *falling heavily on it* while trying to turn.

13   A COINCIDENCE IN NEW YORK

I   1 B   3 C   5 C   7 C   9 B
         2 C   4 B   6 A   8 D   10 C

II 1 She went to the public library *to read a particular poem.*

2 The library was different because you *never see a book on the shelf* there.

3 She had to fill in another form because *they couldn't read the writing* on her first form.

4 It was the *very long crook-like feather on the* old woman's *hat* which *attracted* Denise's *attention.*

5 She said that her *handbag had been* stolen *just* when *she was* getting off *the underground train.*

6 Denise decided to take the old woman to the tea-shop because *she had no money to* get *home* and *she* had had *nothing to eat all day.*

7 She left her handbag *on the chair* near the old woman.

8 She took the address *so that* she could *return the two dollars.*

9 She didn't retrace her steps because she thought it was *too much trouble.*

10 It was a good idea because *all the buildings in New York are centrally heated.*

14 THE TRAGIC STORY OF THE BALLOONIST

I
1 D	3 C	5 B	7 C	9 B
2 D	4 C	6 A	8 B	10 C

II 1 He was famous because he was *one of the* greatest *balloon-masters.*

2 It came as waste material *from a chemical factory.*

3 None. He was *able to do* it all by himself.

4 It was so well counter-balanced that he could lift it with one hand.

5 It *started to go up* because *two sandbags slipped off* the load-ring.

6 They were *in the little hut getting dressed ready to* fly their balloons.

7 No, it wouldn't. He was already very high up and it would have been dangerous to let go.

8   They were never able to find out *what had happened* because Jaeger *was dead when* they *found him.*

9   We know that she knows something about ballooning because Gerry says that she continued ballooning and *has, since* the accident, *filled* Gerry's *balloon.*

10   The balloon eventually *landed quite safely twenty-five miles away.*

15   THE UNFORTUNATE STORY OF THE LOST MONEY

I   1 C   3 C   5 A   7 A   9 C
       2 B   4 D   6 B   8 A   10 D

II   1   He had his unfortunate experience *in North Africa.*

2   He was going *to close* it *up* because he was going *on leave to England for three months.*

3   He *put* the money *under the papers in the top left-hand drawer of* his *desk,* in his *sitting-room.*

4   He wanted it because he *was going into the town to do various things.*

5   He thought that *Idris had taken* it.

6   He *felt guilty* because he was *going through* Idris's *personal possessions* without his permission.

7   He asked them to go *to the house to investigate* the disappearance of his money and, particularly, to investigate whether Idris had stolen the money.

8   *He didn't* show any feelings *at all; he just shrugged his shoulders.*

9   Tom gave Idris some *money* on the day he left because he had not given him *notice* that he was sacking him.

10   It's a *magazine.*

16   A WORRYING EVENING WAITING FOR NEWS

I   1 A   3 A   5 D   7 C   9 D
         2 C   4 C   6 C   8 B   10 C

II   1   *He was going on a business trip to Brussels* for his *company.*
         2   Yes, he had, *several times.*
         3   She was *getting* Catherine, her small daughter, *ready for bed*
             when *the telephone rang.*
         4   She *heard the final words of an announcement,* saying
             *'relatives of passengers please telephone the following
             numbers',* followed by *a list of numbers.*
         5   No, because she was in a state of shock.
         6   She *had seen his air-tickets* and she knew that *he had checked
             in at a BEA desk,* so she thought he was flying on a BEA
             plane.
         7   She thought he had said it would take off *at about six or ten
             past six.*
         8   The exact time of take-off of the crashed plane was never
             given on the news.
         9   Elizabeth's brother *rang the airline.*
         10 The information was *finally* given at *a quarter to ten* when a
             news bulletin was interrupted to give *further* details *about the
             flight.*

17   AN AMUSING DAY ON A BUILDING SITE

I   1 C   3 A   5 C   7 D   9 C
         2 B   4 C   6 B   8 A   10 C

II   1   Ricky found it particularly difficult to run *with a very heavy
             load in a wheelbarrow over planks which had been laid
             across holes.*
         2   *A very heavy load, like wet concrete or something like that,*
             makes the planks sag a lot.

125

3   He *worried about keeping his balance and keeping the barrow on the plank.*

4   The purpose of the extra deep *hole was* to collect *the rain-water.*

5   He saw a *completely grey 'statue' with a shovel in its hand.*

6   Yes, he thought *he was very good* at it.

7   *His hair stream*ed *back* because he was moving fast.

8   He had just wiped some of the first load *out of his eyes and out of his hair.*

9   They saw the Irishman standing there, *completely still, as though* the concrete *had set already.*

10   He *wiped* the concrete *out of his eyes*, looked at the two men and then threw his shovel into the sump before climbing out of the hole.

18   THE HORRIFYING HAPPENINGS AT A STUDENT DEMONSTRATION

I   1 D   3 B   5 C   7 C   9 B
        2 B   4 C   6 D   8 B   10 C

II 1   *The President of the Students' Union had been killed.*

2   They intended to hold *a protest march at* the student's funeral.

3   The *coffin* was kept *on the university campus.*

4   She wanted to collect her *car*, which had been *having something done to it,* so that she could *go away for the week-end* in it.

5   *The garage was about a mile and a half away from her* home.

6   She describes the *atmosphere* as *angry* and *tense.*

7   He wrenched *the lid* of the coffin *open.*

8   They gasped in horror when they discovered *the coffin was empty; there was no-one in it.*

9   Comments like *'The coffin's empty'* and *'The body's gone'* passed among the crowd.

10   He was going *to be buried* in his parents' *village.*

19   THE DRAMATIC EVENTS AT THE BANK

I 1 B   3 C   5 C   7 C   9 C
       2 A   4 B   6 D   8 D   10 D

II 1 Just one man went to rob the bank.
       2 He demanded *three million crowns* and the release of a man from *prison*.
       3 She says that *one was pregnant and the other two were rather old*.
       4 We know that the *whole area* was *cordoned off* and so *nobody could get* near the bank.
       5 They went into *the vault* of the bank and *locked* the door.
       6 Three hostages were women and one was a man.
       7 They planned to get *tear-gas* in through some holes they had *bored in the roof*.
       8 He *tied a noose* of rope round each hostage's *neck*, so that *when the gas came in they would faint* and so hang themselves.
       9 He listened to *the news* on the *radio*.
      10 *No.* He was kept by the police in that town to be *questioned*.

20   THE FASCINATING STORY OF A FIND IN THE ROOF

I 1 A   3 B   5 D   7 B   9 D
       2 D   4 C   6 A   8 C   10 C

II 1 The house is unusual because *it seems to* consist of *three cottages 'knocked together'* to form one house *with a more modern piece* added *later*.
       2 He began to do *alterations to make* the house *more suitable for* their *immediate needs*.
       3 He had to *cut a hole in the ceiling* so that he could get up into the roof to *put a water-tank* in.

127

4   He put *a light* in because he *couldn't work any more* in the roof without a light.
5   He *tried, rather roughly, to pull it down.*
6   It was *about four inches long and three inches high.*
7   *On the envelope* was written: *'A Prize for You. William Turnbull. 1851.'*
8   He *put it in a cigar-box and covered it with cotton wool.*
9   He said that soaking in a *special solution* would *soften* the envelope and *restore some of the fibres of the paper.*
10   The *men* who had built *the house* had *written* the *letter.*